THE EDUCATION MIRAGE

THE EDUCATION MIRAGE

◆

How Teachers Succeed and Why the System Fails

Professor (Emeritus) Ira Jay Winn

iUniverse, Inc.

New York Lincoln Shanghai

THE EDUCATION MIRAGE
How Teachers Succeed and Why the System Fails

iUniverse, Inc.

For information address:
iUniverse, Inc.
2021 Pine Lake Road, Suite 100
Lincoln, NE 68512
www.iuniverse.com

ISBN: 0-595-29142-2

Printed in the United States of America

To all my many former students who, hopefully, learned the art of critical thinking and came to expect nothing less than a civilized dialogue—plus occasional bursts of discovery and laughter—and even a thunderclap or two.

Contents

The Education Mirage—Perspective On The Author, Ira Winn ix

Introduction: The Education Mirage xv

Part I—HOW TEACHERS SUCCEED

CHAPTER 1   The Mirage of Teaching and Learning. 3

CHAPTER 2   Senders and Receivers 9

CHAPTER 3   Lesson-Strategy Planning. 13

CHAPTER 4   I Hear and I Forget: Facts and Learning 24

CHAPTER 5   When to Lecture and When Not To 28

Intermission: Odds and Ends to Think About 33

CHAPTER 6   Body Language and Eye Control 35

CHAPTER 7   Levels of Questioning: Definitional Problems and
Values 39

Wilderness in Silence 45

CHAPTER 8   Critical Thinking, Discussion Leading, and
Case-Study 51

Some Prickly Thoughts on Discussion-Leading 55

CHAPTER 9   Case-Study: How it Aids Teaching 58

1. "Bad Chemistry," Bad Manners, and/or Bad Teaching 63

2. Admissions Policy for the Freshman Class 68

3. The Shrinking Safety Net. 76

4. A Case of "Junk Food". 82

5. A Case of Culture Shock and Immigration Policy. 86

CHAPTER 10   Testing and Grading 92

How Teachers Perform: A Self-Test. 103

Part II—WHY THE SYSTEM FAILS

CHAPTER 11   Reform of Education, TV, and Public Policy 107

High School Reform 111

The School Crisis As a Crisis of Culture 114

Tending the Educational Garden. 118

In Defense of Public Education 121

CHAPTER 12   Critical Consciousness and Lifelong Learning 127

CHAPTER 13   Quandaries and Readiness 133

A Tale of Double Vision: Cochise Jackson's Dilemma. 133

Lamenting Teacher Training. 137

When the Very Young Teach Us 140

CHAPTER 14   At the Core of Higher Education 142

The Environment of Reform 146

APPENDIX   Planning Exercises 149

Comments on the five sample plans: 155

Looking Back—The Closing Of The American Mind 159

Bibliography—The Education Mirage. 167

The Education Mirage—Perspective On The Author, Ira Winn

❖

B.A and M.A. (sociology/social sciences)
University of Illinois, Urbana.
Ed.D., U.C.L.A.
—from letters of thanks and commendation:

- "Winn is vitally interested not only in his subject field(s) but in a wide spectrum of the world around him. On several occasions I have observed him instructing a class. He is dynamic, articulate, and discerning. He is an iconoclast who wants to know why and will challenge students and fellow staff members to think."—D.D. MacLachlan, State College, San Fernando, CA

- "Washington looks dull compared to the La Jolla (Peace Corps training) site. You have made training a very exciting experiment."—B. Boyle, Division of Volunteer Support./"I appreciate the great help you rendered this summer. You are deeply missed already."—H. Scott, Asst. Director, Africa Office of Training, U.S. Peace Corps

- "I take this opportunity to formally thank you for the excellent presentation you made on problem-centered teaching to the faculty, staff and graduate students. Many different disciplines were represented in the audience and your knowledge and enthusiasm was noted by those attending."-—J. Davenport, University of Georgia.

- "Thank you for allowing me to observe your U.S. Government class. I wish I had teachers like you thirty years ago when I went to high school. We recited from memory; your students were learning to think" E. J. Neale, Associate Professor," Los Angeles State College.

- "Your discussion of environmental implications of the world's energy problems had the desired effect: it provoked some of the staff to react vehemently, and all of us to reflect seriously upon your proposal for a fresh outlook. Those who have heard you more often than I confirm that this was the usual fine performance which we can expect from you."—S, Amir, Director, Environmental Protection Service, Jerusalem.

- "Thank you for your participation in the 11th annual Interface conference. "Technology and the University Contracting System" was certainly thought-provoking. Your enthusiasm was most refreshing…in spreading the message that universities must look at factors beyond those that are obvious and superficial before entering into research and development contracts." D. Summers, Electrical and Computer Engineering Technology, Southern College of Technology.

- "In approving Ira's candidacy for the bi-national educational planning team in Brazil, we looked to his apparent penchant for developing new approaches to old problems, which would add a "yeast" element to the team's operations.…He very capably lived up to his advance billing. He proved to be a hard and persistent worker…and proved to be adept at working with educators of a different culture."—R. L. Cardwell, Director, Human Resources Office, Agency for International Development, Rio de Janeiro.

- "Your contribution was top quality in both our eyes and the eyes of the participants as evidenced by the reactions on the evaluation sheet. "One of the few really helpful, practical, alive afternoon speakers we had" was not an uncommon comment. A great job."—R.E. Smith, Center for Research and Education in American Liberties, Columbia University and Teachers College.

- "On behalf of the Global Studies Institute, I want to thank you for participating as keynote speaker on the topic, "Humanistic and Political Aspects of the Global Environmental Crisis." Your presentation received the highest ratings of all the presentations in the Institute program…a wonderful job of inspiring and motivating, and at the end of a very long day." C.A, Sexton, St.. Norbert College, Wisconsin.

- Superior Court of California, County of San Luis Obispo. Certificate of Appreciation: In recognition of contributions to the Court and to the citizens of the county, this certificate is presented to Ira Winn for his services as a participant (mediator) in the Dispute Resolution Program."—J. F. Burke, Presiding Judge and S. B. Sefton, Small Claims Judge Pro Tem.

- "Winn's book, *BASIC ISSUES IN ENVIRONMENT: Studies in Quiet Desperation* is entirely appropriate to the teaching of ecology in general science and biology courses. The excellent stimulating questions in his editor's discussion (sections) and the philosophic breadth and intrinsic interest…make this book perhaps the best value today among the hundreds of environmental readings books available."—T. C. Emmel., Department of Zoology, University of Florida (as reviewed in SCIENCE EDUCATION).

- "I have received nothing but enthusiastic response to your appearance here (on the subject of critical thinking and educational reform). You provided a terrific shot in the arm to our Cleveland High faculty and we do appreciate this." R. Ross, Assistant Principal

- "Thank you for filling my emptiness through learning." Signed, a former student (anonymous)-from a card left under office door

A CHINESE PROVERB

I listen and I forget…

I see and I remember…

I do and I understand!

^^^^^^^^^^^^^^^^^^^^^^^^

Introduction:
The Education Mirage

◆

How Teachers Succeed and Why the System Fails

We are all teachers. At various times, we are called upon to question and explain, to communicate wishes and desires, skills, knowledge and understanding. Some of us are highly successful in these roles, others much less so. When we rise to our teaching best we are inspired to go beyond repeating facts, and instead focus on discovery of new patterns and meanings. We arouse curiosity and enthusiasm.

Even more important than trying to teach is motivating to learn. If you don't believe this, try teaching people who don't care or who are not enthusiastic about the subject matter. Watch as their memory becomes almost inoperable.

Teaching has much in common with acting and selling; you have to put yourself on the line. Think of the architect presenting a plan for a new home or office building, a parent trying to get a child to understand the reason for a rule of behavior, a salesman sharply demonstrating why his product is superior; or the citizens' group lobbying the politician, the film-maker or actor holding an audience's attention, the child explaining the computer to an adult etc. The list is endless.

Yet, ubiquitous as is the teaching act, we tend to think of teaching mainly in terms of formal classroom instruction, to long hours sitting in wooden chairs, while someone with a piece of chalk in hand tells us the facts. Or, worse yet, tells us what to think and the five reasons why. And we damn well better remember them because they will surely appear on the next exam—and just as certainly be forgotten a day or two later. Yes, even this we tend to forget.

Although this book focuses on the classroom, in a larger sense it applies to all of us in our daily lives. It asks: How can we teach more effectively? Teaching has never been easy, and in our technological age, it has commonly become mechanical, a lost art. These dulling patterns die hard, while role models for excellence in

xv

the teaching arts are relatively few, particularly as so much creative talent is drawn off into more lucrative opportunities and professions. For the hundreds of thousands of temporary personnel, commonly run through hurry-up training programs, the shock of a live teaching load is often overwhelming. This is even more the case for young college instructors, who are often left to drift and who all too easily succumb to the delusion that talking is the same thing as teaching.

Relatively few people have a natural talent for teaching. In the face of the many frustrations of the classroom, most teachers have to learn the ropes and slowly develop and nurture motivational strategies and the kind of preparation that matures into a true teaching knack. But many teachers never put it all together and simply stumble along, perhaps flashing briefly, only to yield to anger and burnout; they turn off a generation of learners from the adventure of books and subject mastery. Too bad they cannot admit their mistake much earlier and either take corrective training or move on to other pastures.

No one really gets a handle on teaching effectively until they begin to question their aim as well as the purpose of education. New teachers, as well as more experienced ones, must periodically struggle to review their ways, to break through with fresh insights and techniques for self-mastery as well as classroom-mastery. An openness to forming and solving problems, to collecting interesting materials, to accepting the inevitability of change, and to being of good humor are essential to personal growth as well as teacher effectiveness. Teachers must not allow themselves to be seduced by the modern penchant for panaceas—the latest perhaps being computer-assisted instruction. Computers, like television and visual aids, are an important adjunct, but not the magic key to meaningful and long-lasting educational dynamics. Meaningful reform must always deal with the way we think, with sharpening our ability to make judgments and question facts, definitions and values, not simply with the finding and piling up of ever more mountains of data, however necessary that may be in any given instance. The road to teaching hell is littered with mechanical wreckage.

Nor can one learn to teach effectively by simply reading or listening to explanations and directions, no matter how fine the program or how insightful the writer or speaker. While there are general principles and scientific or artistic truths to be had from education guides, commentaries and texts, it takes a live and active class to take the real measure of what one has learned and what one can teach. Much like swimming, we can be coached successfully if we are open to the idea and if we are willing to get wet.

We teach and learn within the range of our unique personality and background. Patience, compassion and persistence are not always readily available or in abundant supply. Frankly, some people are too nervous and ego-involved or too listless and inattentive to teach well. They reach the limits of patience too easily and fail to motivate the learners. They lack a keen sense of humor—a necessary ingredient of both balance and communication. Such types do not make great teachers or even good ones, although they may well make fantastic learners.

People who are bored with or indifferent to helping others reinvent the proverbial wheel (teaching involves much reinvention and rediscovery) are more interested in wheels than invention.—or so the saying goes. Likely, they are much more involved with projecting themselves, and look askance at the idea of developing curiosity and a questioning outlook in others. They should not be encouraged to become or remain teachers.

Ever on the table is a great pedagogical question: Is teaching solely or mainly a function of sending or giving out information? Or, put another way—-If the learners, by and large, don't "get it", has teaching taken place? We must always ask ourselves how much more interested and knowledgeable the learners could be if faced with the best of teachers? We must also ask whether the quality and importance of the learning is worth the time expended. In all honesty, I cannot separate teaching method from content, for that is a totally false dichotomy with serious negative implications for teaching, learning, and teacher training.

In this book, *THE EDUCATION MIRAGE*: How Teachers Succeed and Why the System Fails, we will deal with issues and problems affecting all levels of education.

We'll assess the current state of education in the United States—from a teacher's perspective! This is not a usual approach to the subject. The direction of educational reform and testing will be probed, and we will examine which are blind alleys as opposed to meaningful change. We'll underscore the great difference between teaching and preaching.

Also, you, the reader, will learn how to sharpen teaching skills, and how to foster critical thinking and enliven the classroom with problem-centered approaches. You will be directly involved in the process of decision-making as you learn how to dissect lesson strategies and more intelligently prepare and grade tests. And all this will make you better able to reach out to parents, administrators, interested citizens and reformers, and educate them about what teaching really can be if freed from its systemic mire.

Another important objective of *THE EDUCATION MIRAGE* is to examine teaching vigor and articulation between higher, secondary, and adult education. Also to challenge traditional pedagogues to move out of defensive posturing. Very complex and difficult educational reform challenges must be faced and approached with an open mind.

Against the glamour and incessant beat of the mass media, education, particularly formal instruction, is ever more commonly viewed as a boring and dead routine. It need not be. The joy of thinking is alive and well in the interactions of the problem-centered class. Passive television is at a distinct disadvantage as compared to dynamic instruction with awakened students. There are practical strategies for reform of education that go far beyond a life glued to electronic boxes and screens. An education based mainly on data gathering, memorization, and regurgitation produces few, if any, creative minds. It is hardly a sound national or local investment.

Data is important, but it needs to be interpreted and analyzed against a foundation of values, and with a sense of direction and purpose. Education must hone judgment for it to be worthwhile and effective. A glut of information is just not the same as a sharpened mind.

Given these concerns, I remain optimistic that we can see and pass beyond the mirage that frames the popular perspective on teaching and learning. We must turn away from the nostalgic dreams, blind alleys and illusions about education that so often convince us that we are "teaching." With all its problems and challenges, we must never forget the thousands of creative and dedicated teachers who successfully command a teaching life and have a handle on motivating learners. In the course of this study we'll probe their strategies and mystique—and unfold approaches to inquiry that mark them as masters of the teaching arts.

I look ahead to a new century, when schools and universities will become more creative and inspiring places. Hopefully, this work will contribute to saving generations of students from apathy and countless hours of boredom and a host of educators from avoidable frustration and burn-out. Perhaps this effort will awaken and salvage only a relatively few teachers and professors and students. In either case, the effort proves worthwhile.

PART I

HOW TEACHERS SUCCEED

1

The Mirage of Teaching and Learning

A mirage results from a failure in perception, either visually (optical illusion), or because of wishful thinking. If teachers would reflect more on their classroom experiences, they would see that much of their effort at educating is based on misperceptions and false assumptions about how students receive information and learn. The illusory perceptions of their teaching role are what I refer to as "the mirage of teaching and learning."

A number of years ago, I sat with some friends in a restaurant known for its fine hamburgers. On opening the menu, we discovered that all the items had clever legal titles, reflecting a location close to the downtown courts. There was a "Bailiff Burger" an "Attorney Burger" and so on. I ordered from this entertaining list a "Justice Burger." When the waitress appeared I said jokingly, "I think I'd like the 'Justice Burger,' but first, by some chance, is this a Warren Burger?" She looked at me bewildered, completely oblivious to the reference I had made to the then present Chief Justice of the U.S. Supreme Court. "What do you mean?" she asked puzzled. Still teasing, I replied, "If it's a Warren Burger, I might find it hard to digest." She still didn't get it.

Some might say that she was not culturally literate or politically attuned. I joked with my friends after she left the table, and we discussed how sad it is that people don't read the newspapers or keep up with national and world events. It bothered me to know that the waitress doubtless had taken a number of history and civic classes in high school, maybe even in college. However, I knew that while she was not on my wave-length, she might be quite knowledgeable and adept, far more than I, about marine biology, fossil ape man, Taoism, architecture, pottery, or even about her own community politics.

I know that it is not easy for people to retain knowledge, as witness the number of teachers who are dependent on their notes. I know that the content of learning is, in the long run, not as important as the ability to think reflectively and be open to new ideas. With that in mind, I'm not too quick to judge people who are drawn to different aspects and varieties of the knowledge tree than I. Much like the pistachio tree, which blossoms and bears fruit in its own long time, we, at best, labor years at cultivation and wisely learn to wait.

Still, we live in a democratic society, and an informed electorate is vital to its progress. I wish all citizens could share in core learning and societal concerns so that we could more intelligently discuss and joke more freely about politics and related issues. It is a dilemma noted by the political analysts Robert E. Lane and David Sears more than thirty years ago. While agreeing that all the evidence shows the informational level of the public is quite low, they conclude "…the significance of information is less in its quantity and more in the uses to which it is put. Pouring *civics* into the electorate won't help much; it won't be remembered long either. Teaching people how to use knowledge, how to conceptualize, appraise evidence, infer causality—there lies a task worthy of a great teacher." Their conclusion most definitely applies to all fields of teaching.

While teaching is our main focus, what we inevitably end up discussing is how people learn and what it is that motivates a desire for knowledge. Long and varied teaching experience has taught me that learning and retention of knowledge is greatly enhanced when a teacher begins with problems rather than with solutions, conclusions and answers. Indeed, there exist illusions about teaching and education that need to be spotlighted here and now, misperceptions that we will return to again and again in various forms in the course of our inquiry:

- *I could be a great teacher if only the students knew more facts.*

  Too many teachers bewail student ignorance, which is then used to justify lesson drills and busy-work assignments. The real teaching question relates to how facts form a meaningful pattern to the learner. In some circumstances, the facts are self evident, but in many more instances, the opposite it true. The jury system is a good analogy. For example, six witnesses to a crime offer conflicting accounts as to what really happened. The jury's job is to make findings of fact.. This is done through deliberations over the problem at hand and eventually a determination of guilt or innocence. They begin with the problem and they end with the facts as best determined from the evidence presented. The problem acts as a sticky framework to which the evidence adheres. Their learning and their judgment is formed by working through the pattern and sifting the facts, *not* by receiving the right answers. Thus, to achieve the educational goal of sharpened judgment, of having knowledgeable students, the process of inquiry, deliberation and fact-finding must be stimulated and encouraged by the teacher. Wise teachers focus on problems.

- *The basket complex:* All too often teachers conceive of the human mind as a basket. The instructor's job is to lob facts into the basket, to fill the container with nuggets of wisdom—the teacher's carefully hoarded gold. The problem is that the baskets all are permeable and a good many have holes in their bottoms. The retention of information is fragmentary, and over time even the best of baskets lose their contents. People who conceive of the human mind as a container make a fundamental mistake, and for a teacher that mistake is deadly. Plutarch summed the problem incisively almost 2000 years ago. He said that the human mind cannot be compared to a pitcher that needs to be filled. Instead it must be viewed as a flame that needs to be kindled and fueled. There is a great difference between the concept of the mind as a container as compared to the mind as a flame. Teachers must spot the illusion of the basket and strive constantly to reject it.

- *Wishing for the good old days:* The third illusion is that there was a golden age of education in the 1950's, and that if we could return to those times, many of our current education problems would be solved. But how *golden* were the fifties? I think back to its stress on conformity—to the man in the gray flannel suit, and to the ferment then boiling unattended in the social fabric of the nation. Not just McCarthyism, the mistakes of the nuclear energy and atmospheric test program, or to the civil rights and racial struggles just then surfacing, but to the very real arguments over the direction of American education in the face of the scientific challenge posed by the success of the Russian space program. Some of the book and journal articles of those times reveal that all was not calm in the world of education: *WHAT IVAN KNOWS THAT JOHNNY DOESN'T* "Can Johnny's Parents Read?"; *QUACKERY IN THE PUBLIC SCHOOLS; COMMUNISM, CONFORMITY, AND CIVIL LIBER-TIES* etc. The *golden age of education* turns out to be a mirage—usually a time whenever it was that *WE* went to school. The kids of today will idealize their school experience when justifying it to their children.

I admire the candor of Clarence Darrow and his memorable commencement address to the 1918 class at Chicago's Senn High School. In typical commencement fashion, an introducer extolled the seniors for their fine education that prepared them so well to go forth into the world. Darrow 's turn came and he won an uproarious admission from the applauding class when he commented, "You're just a bunch of ignorant kids, full of the devil. You haven't learned a damn thing for the four years you've spent here, and you can't fool me because I spent four years in just such a place!" Such were the good old days.

- *Illiteracy is the main problem:* Surely illiteracy is one of our national problems, and not just the inability to read and write, but what is loosely called *cultural illiteracy,* or the lack of common understandings. However illiteracy is defined, the illiterate are much less a threat to our society than the literate It is the highly educated, often the best and the brightest, who pose a far greater danger to society precisely because they sit at the seats of power, and, as history reveals, make decisions inimical to democratic values and to the planet's future. Whether it is the corruption of vested interest politics, the blindness of technological arrogance, or the warping pressures of the human ego, the educated have proven likely to succumb. Enron/WorldCom and similar gigantic financial scandals, the on-going health care crisis, Watergate, Vietnam, the recent Columbia space shuttle disaster all illustrate the failure of our educational system to train wise policy-makers and managers. Cronyism at top levels of government and an unwillingness to tolerate dissenting opinion are signal indictments. The failure to deal preventively and effectively with environmental danger signs is perhaps the best current measure of educational dysfunction. Indeed, the system seems more and more warped toward generating technological fixes and fixers, rather than yielding a generation grounded in humanistic values and one with a broad and long view of problem-prevention.

The delusion that education is a passport to riches, more than an awakening to service for society and stewardship of the planet is disturbing, and dangerous to our future prosperity and happiness. Education must probe and reawaken democratic values, personal commitment, and long range thinking if it is to have much potency and success with either the illiterate or the so-called achievers. Teachers must continually question (and correct) their aim, if the fourth illusion of condescension toward the illiterate is to be fairly balanced and seen for what it is.

Racing to Cover the Curriculum: The fifth illusion results from increasing explosion in the sheer quantity of information. We delude ourselves by thinking that we can somehow cover essential information in every field of study by speeding up and by ever more surface coverage of materials and expanded lists of basic facts for memorization. Because of time constraints of the class hour and the school year (and overload with computer delivery) it is an impossible and Sisyphusian task. Indeed, even when I took history in school during and after World War II, we had barely enough time to get to the 1920's. There has been more history written since 1918 than in the two hundred preceding years. The same knowledge explosion has occurred in every subject field. Some more and some less.. The idea of racing faster and faster through an ever-expanding curriculum is no solution to the problem.

Yet, that is just what we tend to do, denying the obvious and refusing to face up to the need for curriculum reform based on in-depth study of representative issues and problems. Should the penchant for surface coverage and speed-up continue, even with the aid of the new technologies, the teacher of the future might better be trained as a tobacco auctioneer, with an M.A. degree, one able to race the students through the entire curriculum in two semesters. The hapless learners will be droned into insensibility at several times the current rate.

• *Education as quiz mastery:* One final illusion has to do with the tendency to honor the patina of learning— the ability to recall obscure facts and identities as though the whole purpose of education is to produce a successful player at the game of *Trivial Pursuits*. Doubtless, the inability to identify important people and recall core learning are often a worrisome and frustrating sign of inadequate education. But the other side of the coin reveals that there is no necessary correlation between winning accolades for book knowledge and impressive recitation of facts, and being an ethical human being in the larger game of life—or even a wise decision maker and manager.

Few of us today could pass exams in the fields once well studied, but which now are an exercise out of the dim past. And few teachers could pass exams given by colleagues in fields outside their own teaching specialties, although they expect students to do so regularly.

Education is not a quiz show or a preparation for one. The problem with that kind of training is that it negates the primary importance of sharpening judgment, and relegates questions of values and definition to the status of minor objectives. Sharpened judgment is a result of great amounts of time and effort spent working through problems so as eventually to arrive at a pattern of facts that can yield important conclusions. That is akin to what Einstein remarked about imagination being more important than knowledge.

In sum, education is a lifelong process. We can only begin in each teaching hour and in each course of study to stimulate critical thinking and open up learners to development of intellectual curiosity. The worst that we can do as teachers is to blunt their interest in subject and in the adventure of learning. So it is extremely disturbing to find school districts and politicians touting teaching-to-test standards that more often negate or make a hardship of the critical process, meanwhile filling empty teaching slots with minimal cost personnel who are unqualified and usually incapable of stimulating reflective thinking.

The race to capture an academic degree or diploma never really marks completion of education. Rather, it is a measure of inputs, of efforts expended over a given time period. In this sense, there is a fundamental difference between educational gardening and educational decorating. A gardener wants to see the plants grow as a part of long and loving cultivation. The decorator is more interested in form and is likely to bring in full-grown trees and shrubs. Too many people see education from a decorator's reference; they expect that by completion of high school, college, or professional school that mastery will have been achieved. It doesn't work that way. Education is much like planting and growing trees; they take years to develop, sometimes nearly a lifetime to reach full maturity.

I suppose that one day some wit will write a book called, "Is There School After Death?" Some would say that much schooling today is a form of slow death, a stifling of genuine creative pursuit and intellectual curiosity. I'll leave you with that paradox, noting that great teachers work with interesting problems, not mainly with a parade of facts and canned multiple choices. It is true for every field of study. The key is choosing problems that impel critical thinking and that turn the learners on. If you, the teacher, are not turning them on to the adventure of ideas, you are only fooling yourself about education.

2

Senders and Receivers

Basically, there are two types of teachers—*senders* and *receivers*. Senders are primarily concerned with what they are going to tell the class about the subject under study, while receivers are more concerned with the questions they are going to pose. Senders focus on their own ability to explain information and give answers; receivers focus on how the class will process the problem presented and what the learners will contribute to the dialogue by way of judgments and solutions. Senders also concentrate on organizing their notes and lectures, while receivers relate more to organizing inquiry and preparing for active listening. Simplified, senders tell and receivers ask.

Many teachers erroneously view the difference between these two polar teacher types as a matter of the importance placed on knowledge, as though only the senders are concerned with rigorous academic preparation and subject content. In truth, both types of teachers, senders and receivers, are inextricably involved with both content and method, although in very different ways. Indeed, there is sender and receiver in all of us. However, it is also true that the traditional image of the teacher role model is misidentified with sending. Say the word *teacher* and the image comes forth of a man or woman at the front of the classroom, pointing, telling, explaining, or demonstrating, while the student listens, absorbs, and regurgitates. When the traditional sender-teacher signals the class that he is ready to receive, he commonly expects either a question on which he can begin sending answers once again, or a carbon copy answer of what he has just recently told the class.

Let us step back a moment and consider anew the Chinese proverb: "I listen and I forget; I see and I remember; I do and I understand." What senders always forget is that learners only imperfectly remember material set forth in lecture, and that like witnesses to a crime, they all perceive different aspects of the subject and scene. Listening and watching are important, but learning often takes much more than that. The human capacity to absorb and remember is imperfect at best, even haphazard, and is subject to all kinds of perceptual selection and distortion. The reading of a simple page of analysis, to say nothing of a half hour lecture, will easily produce a variety of interpretations of what was said, as well as what was implied. Senders seem surprised by these perceptual deficiencies so obvious in students and they often complain about the inability of today's learners. They fail to see that it has always been so. They forget the long rehearsal hours that went into their own preparation and gloss over their own forgetting rate. They review their notes. They fail to recognize that in the very course of lecturing, the teacher is the only one in the room who is active, and reinforcing his learning by acting as chief learner. Thus the adage, "If you want to learn something difficult to remember, teach it!"

But the measure of teaching is not simply what the teacher does, or how he or she stands and delivers. The full measure of teaching includes what the students receive in the way of improved critical capacity and knowledge—not solely good factual awareness or sharp critical capacity, but both! Teaching implies this full measure of learning, or it makes no sense as an educational activity. Otherwise, it would be like watching a baseball game with an active pitcher but no batter, or listening to a symphony in which there is an active conductor but no orchestra. Some game! Some concert!

Seen in this light, teaching and learning is a mutual process of giving and sharing. Sending and receiving is a balancing process and not a seesaw competition weighted heavily at one end. Great teaching is an opening process for both learner and the learned, and not a closed circuit beginning and ending at the teacher's desk. Thus, the well balanced, artful teacher know full well the value of questioning and uses important questions to focus a discovery process and active involvement by the learners. A true dialogue between learners and teacher, yields a dynamic rhythm that breaks the inertia of traditional sender-type teaching. Only then does teaching become a lively art!

To be a good teacher, one must be in love with questions, even more so than with answers. On first thought, this may seem strange because commonly we think of teaching in terms of giving (and receiving) right answers. Answers are a very important result of the teaching process, a fruit of dialogue and questioning. Memorizing right answers, however, is hardly a high order of thinking, and teachers easily forget the forgetting rate of learners. A good memory can be a valuable asset. But as educator Robert Hutchins reflected, "Conclusions cannot really be understood apart from the arguments whereby they were reached." Questions and problems and the dialogue they inspire form the road to self-development, true understanding, and wisdom.

Of course, there are times for the teacher to speak from authority, (expertise gained from years of study), to clarify the question and provide some explanations. But given the propensity of teachers to fall back on sending, there are many more times for teacher silence—strategic *wait times* used to prompt the inquiry process, allowing thought to jell and be vocalized or written. The analysis of problems and case studies, the opening up of learners to an active process of critical thinking, acts as a catalyst and glue that helps the retention of facts. And now facts become useful tools rather than products spewed forth and soon forgotten. Problem-centered teaching is thus the key to balance between sending and receiving.

Teaching is not a quiz show. The payoff is personal growth and a sharpened mind, not grand cash value prizes. Teaching implies both knowledge of subject matter and skill in the art of questioning and listening. Intense focus on mainly recall knowledge signals that surface skimming has taken the place of inquiry; there is minimal penetration of the arguments set for discussion, or the readings are a summary of conclusions, rather than posing problems. Most textbooks fall into this category. They make bland the dialogue, trivialize the questioning, and set forth opinions or guidelines without a true critical context. This makes a farce of problem-centered approaches. Methodology becomes a fixation, with the class wiggling through a boring hour with little student involvement, and even a pooling of ignorance by both the teacher and the learners.

Opening up students to a truly active and critical learning experience is the mark of effective teaching. Timing is the key to heightening receiving. This requires a constant listening for cues from the learners, and considerable patience in both asking questions and waiting for responses. Silence is often golden. The test for the teacher is this: How can I best stimulate and sharpen the dialogue? The test for the student is: How can I hone my thinking about the problem at hand, rather than wait for the teacher to give out "the right answers"?

Thus, the response to the oft-heard complaint about limited critical capacity of students is not more lectures, more drill, or more "going back to the basics." We have heard enough of that song over the last thirty years to insure stalemate in educational planning and continuing narcolepsy in the classroom. That sorry path, in part rationalization of an older generation imposing its daydreams about the good old days upon the young now in school, yields no effective reform. It is a blind alley, analogous to what Santayana once said of the fanatic, "One who redoubles his effort when he has forgotten his aim."

As more and more adults pour into college classrooms, the weight of their life experience nicely balances the subject expertise of the teacher; it gives impetus to the movement away from over-reliance on standard lecture recitation. Great teachers draw on this well of experience, enlivening relevant classroom dialogue and thereby increasing motivation and sharpening analysis. It forces a crossing of age lines and disciplinary barriers that so often act as blinders to understanding and political awareness.

Discussion will always be the anvil upon which the spark of truth is struck. The pulse of teaching lies more in asking than in telling, in good questions much more than in handing out answers. The telling is the easy part of teaching that can much more easily be taken over by computers and new technology. Inquiry and problem orientation, and particularly discussion will always remain as human arts with the greatest human potential.

The fundamental difference between sending and receiving, or preaching and teaching, is evident in the light of what we know about learning and creativity. The preacher has found the truth and is driven to make you believe; in contrast, the teacher seeks the truth and tries to help sharpen your critical mind.

How many of us are in the right profession?

WHEN THE APPLE FALLS

From the time of the expulsion of Adam and Eve from the proverbial garden of Eden to the modern day Apple Computer, the fruit of the apple tree has symbolized the compelling search to find and to know.

For thousands of years, countless millions of people observed the simple act of fruit falling from trees. But aside from food value, the drop remained somewhat a mystery until the physicist, Isaac Newton, came to draw from that proverbial event an understanding of principles—which from that time on became known as "the law of gravity."

Newton was well-trained and ready to learn. He had an inquiring mind, a deep curiosity, and was a critical thinker and problem-solver. One might say that he had uncommon "common sense."

We cannot all be Newtons. But we can sharpen our minds and perspectives with an education aimed at motivating us to think critically and reflectively about many things that interest us or are a part of our civic duty and pride. *MOTIVATION TO LEARN DEMANDS A PROBLEM ORIENTATION.* Schools and universities must change greatly if education is to have real meaning for most people and for the values of a democratic society.

3

Lesson-Strategy Planning

Lesson planning (class preparation) is viewed as an onerous burden by many teachers. Some instructors are quite hopeless at it. They confuse plans with detailed lecture notes and see the plan process as a make-work assignment for teacher trainers and department chairmen, who are always ready to critique the lesson preparation. New college teachers rarely paper plan, and pay a high price for their dismissive attitude.

In some teaching situations, this kind of bellyaching may have a ring of truth, but it also misses an essential point. That is, planning focused on teaching strategy forces one to think about goals and objectives, how to get the class involved in critical thinking about subject matter, and pointedly how to stimulate participation in dialogue about key questions and problems.

Sometimes lesson planning becomes too detailed and is made a kind of training fetish. There is little evidence that the producers of the most exacting and lengthy plans make for the most creative teachers. Plans that might look great on paper may not work well in classrooms practice. On any given day, what does work well in one class period may not function smoothly at a different hour and with a different group of students. Good lesson plans must have flexibility built into them, and the teacher must become a master at reading his or her class. Planning should always be viewed as a practical guide, not a theoretical construct. Good plans are strategic material that can be used for years before becoming dated; they are even a tradable commodity among teachers in the same field of study. Indeed, sharp teachers often barter good lesson plans.

A strategy-oriented lesson plan is not a minute-by-minute guide to the teaching hour. Nor is it a list of topics for recitation or lecture. Neither is it a vague outline of wishes and long range goals, or even a list of question for the day, (although good questions are an essential part of planning and teaching). *What* then is a lesson strategy plan? Simply put, it is a written preparation for getting the learners involved with a problem! Indeed, if there is no problem on the table for the students to ponder and solve, motivation drops off and passivity take hold. The teacher or professor may orate relentlessly, wave his arms, pace back and forth, think deeply aloud, cite wonderful references, but by and large, the students are out of the boat or on another planet. They have become spectators instead of players, for the real learning has been taken over by the instructor. Lesson strategy planning aims at preventing this from happening!

In order to fully comprehend this point, it is essential that we get into the head of both the teacher and the student. We'll begin by examining the markedly contrasting plans of two teachers in approaching an introductory lesson on vegetable gardening. How does the mental set of teacher "X" differ from that of teacher "Y"? How do their objectives and strategies compare, and what would be the likely outcome for learning?

<u>Teacher X's Plan:</u>

Objective: Show how to get involved in a process of cultivation and values of gardening (sun, nature). As students dig and plant, the paper garden plan develops.

Motivator: Move outside quietly and dig up an area of 30 x 30 feet. Ask class what they need, such as rakes, pitchforks, seeds, poles for pole beans, etc. Begin rows.

Strategy: 1) Are tomatoes better from seed or from nursery plants?
2) Hills or rows for squash and cucumbers?
3) Read the excerpt from seed manual on hints for growers of small vegetable gardens. Ask class for best tips found. (Here I give a short introduction—*10 minutes*

Discussion: I lead to main points today, so class gets the right plan. (Bring out health values of fresh vegetables.)

Evaluation: Ask students if they enjoyed the work. Distribute a model of a small vegetable garden plan the students can take home and use.

Teacher Y's Plan:

Objective: Students will develop a plan for a 30' x 30' vegetable garden. They will plot locations for specific crops and explain their choices using a short pamphlet entitled "Hints for the Small Vegetable Gardener."

Motivator: Does anyone have a vegetable garden at home? (Or know of someone that does?) What are the benefits of maintaining such a garden in the city?

Strategy: Distribute copies of "Hints for the Small Vegetable Gardener," as well as two copies each of a graph paper vegetable plot with a north direction arrow. Students choose five priority guidelines and plot their garden on graph paper while preparing to explain and justify their selections. After 15 minutes:

Discussion: 1) Does the size of the garden raise special problems?
2) Let's imagine that there is no north direction arrow on our working plan. How might that complicate planning?
3) What is "cooperative pairing" and how can it help us plan better? Should tall corn have priority for certain areas of the garden?
*15 minutes to finalize plans and reasons for choices.

Evaluation: Five students present plans to class. Strengths and weaknesses are discussed by the students and later the teacher. Plans are traded or collected for review by teacher. Students are shown the available garden area and told to wear appropriate clothes for tomorrow's garden work.

◆   ◆   ◆

Vegetable gardening is not usually thought of in terms of teacher planning and preparation. But it is for this very reason that it makes a good neutral ground for exploring teacher perspectives and mental set for teaching. Above are two well-intentioned teachers who approach their subject from two completely different perspectives. Teacher "X" strives to get his class out on the ground and working as soon as possible, perhaps before the students even have a clue as to what the lesson is all about. Teacher "Y" is more studied and methodical. He, too, wants the students working on the garden, but not before they have thought out what they are doing. Teacher "X" may get by, despite generating a lot of confusion by the lack of order to his plan, especially if he has a great personality that draws the class along. But his plan is almost an invitation to disaster. His strategy calls for the students to do the reading while they are out digging and one wonders how on earth his students are to do any of their own thinking about vegetable garden planning. Indeed, he gives out a finished model plan without ever finding out what ideas the students have generated for their particular plot of ground. Teacher "X" may in fact be a very good gardener, but his lesson planning shows poor organization and a serious lack of thinking about how learning takes place. His plan is haphazard, although some students will inevitably enjoy the fun part of the gardening. And although he generates lots of (random) student activity, one has to wonder about his preparation. Teacher "X's" 'let's just do it' approach opens the door to considerable and unnecessary student disruption and inevitably lost opportunities for critical thinking.

In contrast to teacher "X", teacher "Y" is very careful to put a problem on the table right from the start. He wants his students thinking about the plan for the garden and involved in a reflective approach to its execution. Each step in teacher "Y's" plan leads logically to the next, and he is very much concerned with students motivation and involvement. He has carefully reviewed the objectives and materials for this introductory lesson and has put himself in the learner's shoes. Also, he could easily trade his lesson with another instructor or substitute teacher in the same field. This could not be said for the plan of teacher "X", which has some nice individual elements, but seems almost scattered and a directionless arrangement that creates confusion and invites too much waste of class time. Having observed too many "X" type teachers operating in the classrooms, I find that around ten percent can pull some order out of the apparent planning chaos, but ninety percent will waste a majority of the class hour with teacher-induced disruption and distractions, and failed attempts to take control and get the class motivated and moving in the desired direction.

Again, I wish to note that teacher "Y", with all his fine planning, may not be able to pull off a good lesson. That depends on many other aspects such as personality, good eye contact, a sense of ease in the classroom, relationships with students, etc. At the very least, he is well prepared. His lesson plan flows logically, and his strategy reinforces his objectives, and the class becomes very much a part of the process of critical thinking.

Teacher "X" is almost entirely a hit or miss proposition. Sometimes he will be able to pull the class along, but more likely he will waste much valuable class time with banter and soliloquies, in orders and counter orders. It is likely there will be little sustained effort at inducing critical thinking by the class. If, in addition to haphazard planning, teacher "X" has problems of personality, eye contact, body language, and ease with students, it is a safe bet that his class will stumble through the hour, and fall into complete chaos on bad days. A better lesson strategy plan, with more thought as to how to get the students constructively engaged in the problem, would bring order and greater productivity to teacher "X's" class.

Now, let's step back and review the key components of a strong lesson plan strategy. Of course, there are perhaps hundreds of model lesson plans available, each with its own areas of emphasis and degree of detail required. Here, I am concerned only with the essential elements for *planning that is problem oriented*. Again, I emphasize that if there is no problem to be addressed, the teacher and the students end up chasing their tails. It is the nature of problems and the questions that flow from them that makes a lesson plan worth writing.

I contend that a solid, problem-oriented plan can and should be put together in about a half an hour or less. Teachers who spend hours and hours writing lesson plans for the next day would be better off reviewing their subject and taking a good walk before sitting down at the keyboard. Undeniably, ideas tend to flow more freely when one is relaxed and not uptight about planning for the next hour or day. Lesson planning is a tool, not a fetish!

Overly long hours expended on planning usually indicates a flawed perspective about lesson strategy. Invariably, that frustrated teacher is fixated on what he or she is going to tell the class about the subject matter. What the teacher needs to do is change perspectives and turn the approach completely around: "How am I to get the problem on the table, and what is the best way to get the students working at solving it?" Even with a lecture (although much less so), there are ways to motivate students to address the problem and to actively participate in solving the question at hand.

Let's examine the basic components of a good lesson plan before actually viewing a few models of strong vs. weak planning. I suggest that the topic of the lesson plan be put in question form and restricted to what the class can cover realistically in one teaching hour. For example, the problem-posing mode is attained by changing from "George W. Bush" to "What did President Bush mean in defining an 'Axis of Evil'?—or from "Food additives in the marketplace" to "Why are food additives so controversial?" Another example: from "Norman Mailer the writer" to "How did Mailer's writing reflect his life?"

There are many variations on these topics. My suggestions serve mainly to demonstrate how to put oneself into a problem-centered setting that will aid in lesson planning. Good topical questions should not easily be answered by students, but should set the stage and tone for an interesting inquiry. By wisely framing the base topic for the hour, the teacher assumes the needed perspective for problem-oriented planning.

Writing Objectives: Well-stated objectives simply and clearly define what learners will be able to do or perform in an hour of class time. These are teaching goals for both students and the teacher, and represent attainable learning outcomes for the short run. Longer range goals and ideals of learning are best left out of the lesson plan, but kept as part of a rationale for a teaching unit (sequential lessons that form a packet of instruction for a week or longer to accomplish). Lesson plan objectives are practical statements of targets for students' performance. For this reason, try to avoid general words such as *appreciate, know, understand, think about*, etc. Such words point to long range learning outcomes important to teaching, but too vague to weigh in a teaching hour. Thus, in objective writing, we move away from the general learning outcomes and define clearly the specific targets. In the following examples, letter "a" signifies a too vague objective, while letter "b" shows a change to an acceptable performance standard:

Here are some examples of end-of-hour outcomes:

THE STUDENTS WILL BE ABLE TO:

vague:	a.	appreciate a healthy diet
pointed:	b.	select and defend the diet that has the lowest fat intake
	a.	get the feel of a computer keyboard and study home keys
	b.	copy a paragraph without error and identify home keys
	a.	know how Elizabethans lived in old England
	b.	write major characteristics of Elizabethan life
	c.	understand which recent presidents were successful
	b.	define standards for presidential success and rate five recent presidents
	a.	ponder the destruction of the Amazon forests
	b.	explain the implications of the Amazon forest destruction

Of course, the vast majority of lesson plans will have more than one objective; perhaps 2-4 per lesson plan would be the normal range. Some will be more difficult to attain than others, but together they should present the learners with a varied and challenging menu.

Some teachers (and administrators) are perplexed and baffled by the task of writing performance objectives. Invariably, they continue to think of learning as mainly what they deliver to the students—or to the teachers in the case of administrators. Again, we must turn our thinking around and accept learning as a two-way street. To achieve maximum effect from learning activities, the learners must be activated and made a primary part of the process. Teaching is far more than telling; learning is far more than sitting passively. Telling and listening are part of the learning ballgame, but it is active engagement in the process of analysis and discussion that brings the runners home.

Setting the Stage: The introduction to a lesson calls for attention. It motivates interest in the topic for the hour, and the opening few minutes of the lesson should put an end to distractions and wandering. It could be a question, a photo, an artifact, or a brief anecdote told by the instructor or the student. It should always be relevant to the lesson topic and not be an aside that invites distraction or mutes curiosity. In other words, it is the entrée that leads to the main course.

Those first few minutes of a lesson are critical to setting forth the feeling tone for the period. I have watched too many teachers fritter away this time in idle banter and disorganized administrative procedures that convey to the class a lack of seriousness of purpose or a lack of direction. The message they send to the learners is a mixture of confusion and a lack of preparation. To cover for this failing, they often assign busy work to eat up time and to silence the learners. When they are finally ready to get the class moving on to something meaningful, they have lost the moment. Then they complain about student's lack of motivation and preparedness. They fail to see how they have modeled the very behavior they so often decry. In contrast, a good "set stage" quickly motivates students' interest in the lesson and conveys an immediate sense of teacher purpose and direction. A sharp opening move prods students thinking and working on ideas and activities supportive of the main exploration of the hour. The test of the worth of any stage setting is to what degree it focuses the class on the problem posed in the lesson. Shortly, we'll view some examples of good "sets" and strategies in the sample lessons.

Strategy: A lesson strategy is essentially a recipe for conducting the lesson. A step by step format outlines the problems, materials, and the procedures for the hour in order to get the work accomplished. A strategy is not a theory or philosophical statement, although there is plenty of philosophy of education underlying it.

When it comes to stage setting for a lesson, or determining a strategy, there is no single "right way"; there is a full range of choices from better to worse. In problem-centered teaching, our major goal is to enhance critical thinking. If you want the students to be involved, the teacher cannot afford to do most of the thinking for them. Thus, it is essential that the materials format the problems, but do NOT present the answers. Because they lead the students to pre-packaged conclusions the vast majority of expository textbooks are not only dulling, but counterproductive.

A wise and ready teacher is a fine collector of problem-oriented materials, whether they are clippings, cartoons, puzzles, articles, films, lab samples or other resources that entice learning. The resourceful teacher learns to collect constantly, using students to help frame lessons and gather new and interesting matter. Notebooks and files need to be regularly upgraded especially in courses that demand currency due to explosive changes in information. Sharp teachers learn to trade lesson plans and materials with each other in order to avoid exhaustion, and to keep themselves and the students on their toes and abreast of developments and changing viewpoints in their subject field. Especially given the pressures of large classes and often difficult preparations, it makes no sense for teachers to fail at keeping a resource and lesson plan file for each course, saving the proven best and adding new problem approaches each teaching year. Problem-centered approaches should focus at least fifty percent of every course of study. As the teacher matures, instruction becomes easier and ever more enjoyable as the habits of critical thinking and strategy planning develop almost automatically. The resource file of problem-centered materials assures continuity and variety, and is readily available. True, master teachers will not need to depend so heavily on detailed written plans, particularly as they have internalized the process of lesson preparation. However, for the vast majority of newer teachers, and for anyone struggling hard to develop sharp lesson planning strategies, it is the better part of wisdom to put down on paper and analyze each day where they are going with the class and how they are to get there.

Here are some key question worth asking as one sets forth a plan and strategy:

1. Is the lesson worth doing? (Hopefully is does not condescend or belabor the obvious, but raises important issues.)

2. Does the strategy lead to the lesson objectives?

3. Could critical thinking better be developed using a different approach or materials? Are the materials relevant and problem-oriented?

4. Is it a "best effort" at motivating and involving the learners?

5. Is there good order or sequence that allows the lesson to unfold with minimum confusion?

6. Are the plan, the strategy, and the materials easily understandable and usable (user-friendly) to another teacher within that field of study? How about the clarity for a substitute teacher?

Unless you can answer "yes" to the above six basic questions, you might wish to re-think your lesson.

<u>Questions for Discussion</u>: It is best that each lesson plan include three good discussion questions pertaining to the topic. I suggest only three, so as to avoid the tendency to turn the lesson plan into a page of questions. The skilled teacher will always think in terms of problems and questions, some arising impromptu in the course of class activities. The purpose of having a discussion section in the lesson plan is to foster a questioning attitude during both the writing of the plan and during its implementation A good discussion question forces everyone to think deeply and begin to probe the topic and the material. "Who were the first five presidents?" is not a good discussion question, since it mostly involves a short recall, and holds no potential for the students to get involved in reflective thinking. (How might this question be changed to enhance discussion and analysis?)

The three questions for discussion set down in the lesson plan should be simply put and not be overly long and detailed. Their goal is to help create a framework for inquiry, an atmosphere in which the inquiring mind thrives. Again, the teacher has to be ready to let go a bit and pose these questions not to trick the class or to use them as a platform for expounding his or her own ideas and answers. Rather, good discussion questions are a most effective teaching tool for creating student involvement, penetration of the material, and a first-hand knowledge of what it means to weigh and consider facts and ideas. Weighing and considering are the basis of a democratic and free marketplace of ideas, as well as the hallmark of meaningful and effective teaching and learning.

<u>Evaluation:</u> Toward the end of each teaching hour, there should be time set aside to summarize important learning and to ascertain to what degree progress has been made toward reaching the lesson plan objectives. This can be done in a variety of ways, including student reports, wrap-up questions or problems that press the learners to summarize meanings, a short written exercise, or other kinds of summations that yield feedback about progress or lack of it. Some teachers are quite quick and skillful at this, and gain good knowledge of student progress and the efficiency of the lesson plan simply judging student motivation, productivity, and enthusiasm toward the learning. Other teachers will desire more solid objective evidence most of the time. Whichever the case, feedback and wrap-up are important not just as a summary of learning during the hour, but also as a rein-

forcement of one lesson and the transition to another. A good evaluation should not take up more than a few minutes and may grow naturally out of the strategy section of the daily plan. Or it might involve additional work outside of class. Again, we'll see examples of evaluation devices in the lesson plans that follow.

1) a topic put in problem-posing form

2) objective(s) aimed at specific learning outcomes

3) a motivator that introduces and sets the stage

4) a defined strategy (and materials) for carrying the lesson toward the objectives

5) three good discussion question

6) a short evaluation that concludes the lesson and gives some indication of he learner's understanding and progress.

Note that in the course of implementing the plan, the students might also set some objectives. Each section of the above framework should not be viewed as segmented from every other section. A lesson either flows or doesn't flow depending on how it is presented by the teacher and by a host of other factors affecting student behavior and interest. The sharp teacher always enters the class fully prepared, but also ready to shift gears and innovate in the face of unusual or unforeseen circumstances. This is not meant to imply a regular excuse for junking the lesson plan and going off the cuff as some teachers are inclined to do. Rather, it underscores the importance of thinking through the lesson plan and standing ready to use it in an innovative way as circumstances develop. Good plans work. They are a key resource for the teacher that, over time, REDUCES the stress of finding workable approaches to better student performance. The practice of good lesson planning should become ingrained early in the teaching career until it becomes so automatic that the teacher always thinks in terms of problem-orientation. Some teachers will find this much easier than others. In any case, it is well worth cultivating the habit and aiming at lesson plan preparation in less than half an hour. The more problem-centered the teacher, the faster the practice will catch on and be perfected. Planning should flow very quickly once the teacher realizes that the work of learning is a natural process of discovery by students and teacher and not a one-way street of cramming pre-set conclusions into the class hour.

Some veteran teachers will have internalized the planning process to the point where, with relatively few notes, they can think through and carry out the plan smoothly and effectively. But for the vast majority of teachers, including veterans, it is the better part of wisdom to maintain a written plan record that can always be referenced and built upon. For the young teacher fresh out of college, perhaps with a few years experience, my advice is not to try to build the Golden Gate bridge from plans carried only in the head; even the best architects commit their ideas and hopes to paper.

At this point, we will move on to other important topics. However, an Appendix has been created for working teachers and trainees especially and those who wish to sharpen their skill at further analyzing lesson plans and strategies. Turn to the end of the book and work through Appendix, beginning on page 149.

4

I Hear and I Forget: Facts and Learning

The great mathematician and philosopher, Immanuel Kant, drew from his work a dictum vital to both science and education: "Theories without facts are empty; and facts without theories are blind." Though facts are essential to learning, in and of themselves, they are simply the raw material of mental labor and production. That is indeed a fact—and one which teachers must learn to use as a guiding principle. Yet, much teaching proceeds on the false assumption that a substantial pile of facts accumulated and inventoried means that ninety percent of teacher's jobs are done. Far from it! The simple truth is that a point is quickly reached in the class hour where the piling on of facts clutters the scene and turns educational focus away from critical thinking.

Facts are the building blocks of every subject, and obviously there can be no education without reasoning based on facts. But teaching fixated on student recall quickly loses direction and vitality; tidal waves of data drown out or obscure meaning, priority, value and relevance. The evidence is plain to see in surveys of student and voter knowledge, and many a report on education has long lamented this sorry condition. When facts are made an educational fetish, learning becomes mainly an exercise in regurgitation. This leads to more surface skimming in order to collect ever more data, even as student passivity and apathy becomes evident. A course based mainly on learning facts is much like forcing down a tasteless meal; it is best quickly forgotten. Teachers, who more often than not, refuse to face the educational implications of what they agree is a major problem, readily acknowledge the lack of retention by students of even basic information. Imagine the outcry from professors and teachers if they had to take periodic certification examinations covering detailed information in several subjects outside their major fields of study—subjects they once passed in school and which they thought lie conveniently behind them.

An outpouring of facts makes for an impressive display, and gives at least the appearance of learning to the person who has soaked up the information. But many people who possess virtual volumes of information are at a loss in knowing how to use it, or how to put it all together. The *best and the brightest*, with years of elite education, still led us into the Vietnam war, exported our auto and steel industries, piled up mountains of debt, and still make decisions proving hurtful to long run economic vitality and the social cohesion of the country. Possession of multitudinous facts is no guarantee against reaching erroneous conclusions!

A lack of information and facts is an even greater curse. People are then at the mercy of forces which they neither comprehend nor perceive. Those who lack factual knowledge are at a loss at what to say or do, and they are plainly embarrassed. Ignorance is hardly bliss. There is no doubt that knowledge and information are very important, especially in our technological age. But as Einstein wisely concluded, "Imagination is more important than knowledge." The poet Edna St. Vincent Millay mulled this truth in an incisive sonnet:

...Upon this gifted age, in its dark hour

Rains from the sky a meteoric shower

Of facts...they lie unquestioned, uncombined.

Wisdom enough to leach us of our ill

Is daily spun; but there exists no loom

To weave it into fabric...

No loom. Indeed, no weaver! Yet, the purpose of education is to make of us weavers, and not misers who collect facts simply as a way of display and hoarding.

Without being able to draw meaning from a body of facts, to weave patterns and hypotheses and accurate conclusions, all the facts in storage are little more than gas in the ground—a potential source of energy, but an inert mass for all intents and purposes.

Teachers commonly make the mistake of trying to motivate learning by discussion based on recall of information. This is a dead end, for fact recall exercises do not really constitute discussion and at best are but a primitive part of inquiry; at worst, they are a dulling type of drill conducive to apathy and stupor. Teacher effort is much more effectively aimed at working cooperatively with learners in quickly laying key facts on the table in the context of a problem; then the major effort is directed at figuring out which facts are needed or missing, what are the conditions, which elements are most important, and what is valid or invalid?

Ultimately the process of discussion must focus on other kinds of questions calling for judgment of values and definitional problems.

Facts must be culled and arranged as the raw material of discussion, but not as an end in themselves. Further, facts need a framework of magnets on which to gather and hold, the most effective being the case study or problem situation. *People remember facts when they use them in explaining and trying to solve a problem.* That is why a person can readily explain even a complicated story dealing with a happening at work or on the sports fields, but has so much trouble recalling, say, a sequence of world history or other body of facts presented purely as a narrative chronology. Certainly it helps explain why many a young learner with a supposed difficulty in mathematics has little trouble figuring out a batting average, or what you owe him by way of payment for work.

Oft heard is the argument that learners need ALL the facts before they can hold a good discussion or inquiry session. That is the common excuse teachers give for relying so much on telling and explaining. But it's an exercise in futility, more a fear of losing control, for teachers are among the quickest to forget the forgetting rate, their own as well as that of the students. To the traditional teacher, there are somehow never enough facts to begin the dialogue and so the teacher must continually dominate the discussion.

The lecture becomes endless even as the students become ever more passive. Thus the fact-splattering approach becomes a parody of learning and of problem solving, to say nothing of the democratic process. It is as if the teacher has piled on the ground all the many materials (facts) that go into the building of a house, but fails to allow or involve the learners in the process of design and construction; at long last, he turns them loose to build. Needless to say, the prospective homeowners will be left out in the rain.

In sum, there are two ways of looking at the place of facts in teaching. The first, unfortunately the most common, is viewing the brain as a storage receptacle such as a computer. The teacher's task is to load the damn thing with data and program it for retrieving as large a quantity of information as rapidly as possible. That the human mind is not a computer or is much more than a computer is simply a heresy not to be admitted. In this scheme, endless factual liquid is to be poured from the teacher's bucket into the learner's storage. Function is viewed as less important than form, and the forgetting rate is conveniently forgotten.

The second view of the importance of facts in teaching takes a much more dynamic and conservative tack. Enough facts to start an inquiry process are rather quickly put on the table, with the learners an active part of the fact-gathering and evaluation process. This view rejects the concept of education as a filing service dealing with empty slots and machine-like memory. Instead, it is a critical thinking model remarkable for its exercise of judgment and its culling of information. Again, we return to the dictum laid down by Plutarch almost two thousand years ago:

> "The mind cannot be conceived as a pitcher that must be filled. It must be seen as a flame that needs to be kindled and fueled."

5

When to Lecture and When Not To

We lecture for the inspirational value and because it is a good way to organize and summarize thinking on a topic or theme. With a fine lecture, we share an intellectual adventure with a master, who inspires us with both delivery and oration and by the clarification and integration of knowledge. But it is much like sailing as a passenger on a great ship; one can cross the ocean dozens of times under the best of captains and still not learn very much about the engine room or navigation.

We come away from a great lecture inspired with ideas and a feeling of knowledge and growth. But the human mind is in as much need of active exercise as the body. Listening and watching is not enough. A few hours or days later, the audience is unlikely to remember much of what was said. For a lecture delivered dryly, the memory might be half an hour or less. It has been observed that Sunday sermons rarely have an effect beyond Sunday. Why then lecture at all?

The virtue of the lecture approach lies in the potential for quick summary and clarification. Therein lies a weakness too, the temptation to endless monologue and the tendency of the audience toward passivity and even narcosis. The chief learner in the lecture hall is rarely a member of the audience; it is always the teacher who is the active agent from beginning to end. We are speaking here of an outstanding lecturer, or even just a good one, and not the huge numbers of professors and teachers who rely on reading their notes. The latter group far more readily put their students into a state of apathy or dreamland.

Especially in an age of quick print, the lecture can be an important part of the setting of the stage for learning. We need to remember that the lecture system became entrenched in the schools and universities even before the age of the printing press. Today, lecturing could be entirely bypassed through the use of duplicating print machines, videotapes, and computer hook-ups. But there is still something very special to be had from a live actor thinking on his feet. That is why the legitimate theatre is still with us despite the movies and television. The lecture is a kind of theatre that, well performed, can be a vital role model for integrative and critical thinking. The good lecturer demonstrates reflective teaching, something sadly lacking today when so many leaders depend on teleprompters and a diet wholly prepared by pollsters and hucksters.

Good lecturing and active listening are part of what Alfred North Whitehead described as the romance of learning (curiosity plus inspiration). Together they lubricate the tedious process of piecing things together in order to present and solve a problem (the stage of precision). But teachers, even more so professors, tend to over-rely on lecture. They abuse the approach by wholly dissecting the problem for the students and then "solving" it.

Often they fail to motivate the class, simply because of static delivery or by hogging the stage and drowning out useful, if disparate, ideas. They can inhibit questioning by giving snap answers or drowning the questioner with another round of monologue. Some teachers simply put out the fires of curiosity by their egotistical need to show students just how much they know. They forget that their task is to motivate and inspire learners, even prod them, to a point where they have to do good thinking on their own. In the teaching-learning game, the team leader must not hog the ball.

The good lecturer walks a fine line between his own need to make a presentation and his duty as a teacher to develop his students' critical capacity. The real educational role of lecture, so readily forgotten, is to set the stage for learning, never to conclude the learning process by doing the thinking for the learners. A fine lecturer raises problems and issues, brings focus on salient facts, plays with the possibilities and thereby entices his audience, reaches some tentative conclusions, and most importantly, motivates his audience to question and judge. In this sense, the lecture sets the stage for learning in discussion, it becomes a way of clarifying those questions which will arise in discussion and which will need to be mulled and chewed in a continuing process of inquiry. Too much has lecture become an end in itself, a static and passive process, described by some wag as transferring pencil tracings from the notebooks of the instructor to the notebooks of the students without passing through the heads of either.

So when does one use lecture profitably? There are times when a teacher needs to lecture by way of clarification, or to present certain facts that are not readily available to the learners. A lecture can be a marvelous way to motivate interest in a topic and to inspire the students to go on learning. (It is ironic that so often the word "lecture" is preceded by the words *dry* or *dull*.) A good lecture is also a way to offer special insight by an expert into a complex problem. It is an easy way to make transference from one topic to another seemingly unrelated. Sometimes, a clever and witty lecture is simply entertainment or a way to get something off the teacher's chest. These are all legitimate uses when kept within prudent bonds. But when lecture becomes over-extended and confused with *covering material*, the entire educational process becomes distorted and counter-productive.

"What are you doing in class today, Professor Snerd?" "Oh," he answers, "I am going to cover the volume of cylinders, the Civil War, nuclear fusion, Elizabeth Barrett Browning, or pharonic dynasties." Careful. Likely is it that Professor Snerd will not be presenting a problem in one of these areas for his students to puzzle on, but will be using the full class hour to *go over* a list of items he wants to be sure to *mention* to the learners. What professors and teachers so often forget in their drive to feel satisfied that they have touched all the bases in a course of study, is that there is a world of difference between running through a list of items on the one hand, and offering their students a genuine learning experience on the other. Under the press of time, they justify the common practice of surface skimming.

Here lies the fallacy: Genuine learning involves not simply recalling and repeating information, but being able to apply information, to use it to solve problems. Learners are unlikely to go beyond recall unless they have actively exercised their own reflective and critical capacities. The lecture will have actually wasted much valuable class time if the net result of the coverage is merely some recall of terms and associations that could just as easily been copied from a book. Thus, simply because a student can learn to recognize Elizabeth Barrett Browning as a 19th century English poet, or can name three pharaohs of Egypt, it is no measure whatsoever of his understanding of Browning or her poetry, or the nature of life in Egypt under those three pharaohs. The ability to analyze and reflect on such understandings is cultivated less by lecture and more by student participation. The good lecturer can certainly start the ball rolling with an interesting overview of the subject, but surface skimming has its decided limits—it does more for the teacher's ego than for the students' education.

The most frequent defense of the lecture-fixated teacher or professor is that the students don't know enough to discuss the subject intelligently. Yet, while there is often truth to this claim, it also is a rationalization and reveals a fundamental misperception of the role of education. Students, almost by definition, will never know enough. We are all students, including the teacher. A basic problem can be rather quickly put on the table by the lecturer to start the inquiry process. In the course of dealing with the problem or issue, the learners and the teacher together amass a body of content and sculpt it into useable form. Here the teacher must decide what to contribute and what to leave out for the students to discover for themselves. The work is both process and content oriented, for the teacher or professor is modeling a critical and reflective approach as much as teaching a subject matter. For the instructor to solve all the problems for the students is as educationally absurd as the actions of a parent in expecting a growing child to absorb parent EXPERIENCES by listening to parent lectures about life growing up. People learn best by learning to think for themselves. This includes listening skills, of course, but it also includes the freedom to experiment and make mistakes and profit from them. The teacher or professor, operating at his or her best, can offer background and model reflective thinking. Beyond a point most often reached before the half hour, the wise lecturer guides the learners into a more active process of critical thinking.

Good lecturing is an art. It involves a great sensitivity to the audience and an ability to put oneself into the learner's shoes. It involves skill at raising issues and instilling curiosity, in asking questions and using incisive examples and humor to make the subject come alive and unfold with great clarity. It also means knowing when to stop talking to allow the thoughts to penetrate and further questions to form and motivate the learners. Teachers are simply mistaken if they assume that teaching is talking and learning is just listening. If that were so, schooling could begin and end with little more than tape recorders and note pads. The game of education is far too important and complex for that.

The true art of lecturing is for some people a natural talent, while for most it is best learned by practice with videotaping and under the guidance of a master teacher. There are a few bits of advice that may sharpen focus and help organize material. First, I would ask myself what the learners could gain from my lecture that could not be had from reading or a discussion. How can I tantalize them to think deeply about the issues and what doors can I open for them so they can better think critically about the subject? Secondly, I always think back to that old adage to speakers about establishing guideposts for clarity: "Tell them what you are going to tell them; then tell them; and, finally, tell them what you told them." Remember, lecturing to students is not inoculation! It's more like guiding people up a mountain. One moves ahead and waits. The guide demonstrates and motivates. He waits some more. The learners gradually gain confidence and move on up ahead. You can't do it all for the learners, but you can show them the path. The lecturer is most effective at those ripe opportunities to clarify a complex situation, and then end with a question.

In lecture, as in farming, there is a time for planting and a time for harvesting. In between there is a lot of hard work cultivating the ground. The wise lecturer knows what to plant and when to harvest; he also knows how to work with his students to get them to cultivate and grow. He knows when to start and when to stop. As the sage reporter and confidant Louis Howe told unconfident and ungainly Eleanor Roosevelt as she began to learn the art of public speaking, "Have something to say. Say it. And sit down." To which we might add for the benefit of many a teacher, put it on the table, <u>accept silence, and wait</u>—and wait some more.

Intermission: Odds and Ends to Think About

- In 2001, the Colonial Williamsburg Foundation surveyed teenagers about history and Independence Day, and found that more than 20 percent of respondents did not know from which country the United States had declared independence. Some 14 percent named France. And about 25 percent of the teens were not aware of who fought in the American Civil War.

- In a 1945 postwar poll by National Opinion Research Corporation, it was found that only 21 percent of Americans could correctly answer this question about the Bill of Rights: "Do you know anything it says?"

- In a poll of college seniors graduating in 2000, more named Ulysses Grant (rather than George Washington) as the general who defeated the British at Yorktown in the final battle of the Revolutionary War.

- The front page, headline story in THE SACRAMENTO BEE, July 22, 1984: **Back to Basics Teaching Flunks, Educators Say.** "Back to basics has backfired. The movement trumpeted…as the answer to plummeting test scores has turned out a generation of inadequately educated children, lacking the intellectual tools to make sense of the world around them, according to California educators interviewed by the BEE." Back-to-basics (with its "emphasis on drill, memorization and mass-produced workbooks") has been an "over-simplified and grossly insufficient response to the educational problems that preceded it…As a result, more students than ever before can read, but without understanding or enthusiasm; can write with mechanical precision, but without imagination or inspiration; and can recite arithmetic tables, but without knowing how to apply them."

- Finding ways to bolster teaching skills is more important than improving achievement test scores, which may lead to superficial reform and only short term gains. In a huge study conducted by North Shore Chicago suburban schools, already some of the best-performing in the nation, strategies for school reform were based on years of analysis of how topics are actually taught in those districts and in the U.S. compared to the highest performing school systems worldwide. Several conclusions: "Assign less homework. Throw out the overhead projector (use the chalkboard) Teach lessons well the first time and stop reviewing them year after year. Give teachers more time away from the classroom to improve their skills. Videotape teachers' lessons and critique their performance." Also, reach out to the community to gain support for reforms. Too often, the study concluded, researchers have little understanding of classroom realities. Policymakers have unrealistic expectations of student performance, and do little to help teachers reach expected learning goals. There simply are no quick fixes.

- "Problem-posing education affirms men as beings in the process of becoming—as unfinished, uncompleted beings in a likewise unfinished reality...men know themselves to be unfinished (and) are aware of their incompleteness. In this incompleteness and awareness lie the very roots of education as an exclusively human manifestation. The unfinished character of men and the transformational character of reality necessitates that education be an ongoing reality."—Paulo Freire PEDAGOGY OF THE OPPRESSED. (New York) Continuum: (anniversary edition) 2000 (1970).

something very special to be had from a live actor thinking on his feet. That is why the legitimate theatre is still with us despite the movies and television. The lecture is a kind of theatre that, well performed, can be a vital role model for integrative and critical thinking. The good lecturer demonstrates reflective teaching, something sadly lacking today when so many leaders depend on teleprompters and a diet wholly prepared by pollsters and hucksters.

Good lecturing and active listening are part of what Alfred NorthWhitehead described as the romance of learning (curiosity plus inspiration). Together they lubricate the tedious process of piecing things together in order to present and solve a problem (the stage of precision). But teachers, even more so professors, tend to over-rely on lecture. They abuse the approach by wholly dissecting the problem for the students and then "solving" it.

Often they fail to motivate the class, simply because of static delivery or by hogging the stage and drowning out useful, if disparate, ideas. They can inhibit questioning by giving snap answers or drowning the questioner with another round of monologue. Some teachers simply put out the fires of curiosity by their egotistical need to show students just how much they know. They forget that their task is to motivate and inspire learners, even prod them, to a point where they have to do good thinking on their own. In the teaching-learning game, the team leader must not hog the ball.

The good lecturer walks a fine line between his own need to make a presentation and his duty as a teacher to develop his students' critical capacity. The real educational role of lecture, so readily forgotten, is to set the stage for learning, never to conclude the learning process by doing the thinking for the learners. A fine lecturer raises problems and issues, brings focus on salient facts, plays with the possibilities and thereby entices his audience, reaches some tentative conclusions, and most importantly, motivates his audience to question and judge. In this sense, the lecture sets the stage for learning in discussion, it becomes a way of clarifying those questions which will arise in discussion and which will need to be mulled and chewed in a continuing process of inquiry. Too much has lecture become an end in itself, a static and passive process, described by some wag as transferring pencil tracings from the notebooks of the instructor to the notebooks of the students without passing through the heads of either.

So when does one use lecture profitably? There are times when a teacher needs to lecture by way of clarification, or to present certain facts that are not readily available to the learners. A lecture can be a marvelous way to motivate interest in a topic and to inspire the students to go on learning. (It is ironic that so often the word "lecture" is preceded by the words *dry* or *dull*.) A good lecture is also a way to offer special insight by an expert into a complex problem. It is an easy way to make transference from one topic to another seemingly unrelated. Sometimes, a clever and witty lecture is simply entertainment or a way to get something off the teacher's chest. These are all legitimate uses when kept within prudent bonds. But when lecture becomes over-extended and confused with *covering material*, the entire educational process becomes distorted and counter-productive.

"What are you doing in class today, Professor Snerd?" "Oh," he answers, "I am going to cover the volume of cylinders, the Civil War, nuclear fusion, Elizabeth Barrett Browning, or pharonic dynasties." Careful. Likely is it that Professor Snerd will not be presenting a problem in one of these areas for his students to puzzle on, but will be using the full class hour to *go over* a list of items he wants to be sure to *mention* to the learners. What professors and teachers so often forget in their drive to feel satisfied that they have touched all the bases in a course of study, is that there is a world of difference between running through a list of items on the one hand, and offering their students a genuine learning experience on the other. Under the press of time, they justify the common practice of surface skimming.

Here lies the fallacy: Genuine learning involves not simply recalling and repeating information, but being able to apply information, to use it to solve problems. Learners are unlikely to go beyond recall unless they have actively exercised their own reflective and critical capacities. The lecture will have actually wasted much valuable class time if the net result of the coverage is merely some recall of terms and associations that could just as easily been copied from a book. Thus, simply because a student can learn to recognize Elizabeth Barrett Browning as a 19th century English poet, or can name three pharaohs of Egypt, it is no measure whatsoever of his understanding of Browning or her poetry, or the nature of life in Egypt under those three pharaohs. The ability to analyze and reflect on such understandings is cultivated less by lecture and more by student participation. The good lecturer can certainly start the ball rolling with an interesting overview of the subject, but surface skimming has its decided limits—it does more for the teacher's ego than for the students' education.

The most frequent defense of the lecture-fixated teacher or professor is that the students don't know enough to discuss the subject intelligently. Yet, while there is often truth to this claim, it also is a rationalization and reveals a fundamental misperception of the role of education. Students, almost by definition, will never know enough. We are all students, including the teacher. A basic problem can be rather quickly put on the table by the lecturer to start the inquiry process. In the course of dealing with the problem or issue, the learners and the

6

Body Language and Eye Control

Eye movement and body posture greatly affect the classroom teacher's success at motivating discussion and maintaining the flow of student participation. Of course, there are other factors such as questioning strategy, which are also key to effective discussion leading. But body language and eye movement (usually lack of movement) are factors little understood by most teachers and grossly underestimated in terms of effect on the class. Indeed, most teachers are unconscious about the hidden messages they are sending their learners, especially during attempts at leading discussion.

Watch a teacher carefully during the class discussion session, and the chances are very great that he will immediately fix eye contact on the first student responding to a question. The student then almost naturally responds directly to the teacher rather than to his fellow students. Yet, with practiced eye movement, the teacher can help the learners to respond to each other. More on that in a moment. For now it is enough to be aware that because of teacher eye fixation on whoever is responding at that moment (what I call "eye one on one"—eye 1:1) the pattern of discussion in the class almost always and repeatedly goes back to the teacher, who then seems to feel he has been invited by the class to make a comment or give a short lecture about the point under consideration. Thus a true discussion among the learners does not come to pass.

Instead, discussion flow follows a jerky path of 1) teacher asks a question; 2) one or two students respond; 3) teacher comments or gives short lecture; and 4) back to "start," with another question drawing minimum student input. The learners have grown accustomed to this pattern and have, for the most part, dropped out of the process. They realize that each question is but an introduction to a mini-lecture, with perhaps a very few student volunteers to respond; the teacher will take over the process and soon answer or elaborate on his own questions.

Many teachers are enamored of this process for it gives them a sense of power and control under the guise of leading an open discussion. They justify their authority on the grounds of minimal participation by students who, by and large, are not prepared to discuss the subject at hand. They claim that it is only natural that the teacher should inform them. Rarely do they ponder the reasons for student silence.

Most teachers who admit to difficulties with student participation estimate that in an hour class with 30-40 students, perhaps four or five learners can be expected to actively discuss. By comparison, a really sharp discussion leader with a similar size class can readily get 70 percent or more of students involved in the dialogue during the teaching hour.

This leads us to the problem of faulty eye contact and improper body language. In growing up, we have learned that it is polite and expected behavior to look into the eyes of the person speaking. "Look at me!" the mother tells the child, the wife tells the husband, the salesman tells his customer. Perhaps not in direct commands but in a way that instruction is implied. Direct eye contact tells the speaker that you care about what I am saying and you are making an attempt to hear and validate me. But what goes well for polite or intimate conversation simply proves counterproductive to effective discussion leading!

A classroom discussion is NOT a conversation between the teacher (the discussion leader) and one or two students. Rather, it is a dialogue involving the entire class. Every question thrown on the table by the discussion leader is a question for the whole class. And every response to that particular question is open to comment, agreement, or counter by every participant.

The leader's task is to bounce the learner's response back to the other students so the discussion ball is in good part in their hands. In this sense, the discussion leader has special role responsibilities, more a clarifier and a coach than a traditional pedagogue. The court game is managed by very careful and practiced use of eye movement, with nodding interest to the student responding, while searching the faces of the other students.

The effective discussion leader is not looking for an excuse to take over the game, but is seeking to find out who else wants to play the ball; even as he is carefully listening to the points made by a responding student, he is watching the faces of the class for signs of the urge to participate. Gestures of puzzlement, concern, agreement or disagreement and musing are important facial clues to passing the ball to the next participant. If the teacher is not attuned to these signals, golden opportunities will be lost and the discussion will die. At the same time, he guides the flow to stay on the subject.

Eye contact to the student speaking should be ever casual and polite, but never fixed. Should the student speaking insist on staring only at the discussion leader, it may be necessary for the leader to casually move away or turn the upper body as if to bounce the verbal "shots" back to the rest of the class. The message soon gets through: It is the learner's job to speak to the whole class, and it is the teacher's job to avoid dominating the discussion. It is a delicate balancing act in which both teacher and learners sharpen their ability to listen and to participate.

This does not mean that the discussion leader cannot add some pertinent thoughts or call time out for clarification or order. But it does mean limits to continual teacher dominance, which inevitably leads to learner withdrawal from active participation. The discussion leader does have a serious obligation to penetrate the material and problems under study. In part, this is set up by judicious selection of problem-posing readings or films. Also, by consciously motivating the class, using encouraging and neutral comments to prod discussion: "Interesting!" "How about that?" "Could someone summarize what was just said?" "Anyone else care to comment?" "Supposing…" etc. Such interjections help move things along and are useful in picking up a missed or lost point…but not as a pretext for creating a patter of mini-lectures. Remember, wait-time is critical and teachers must learn to USE silence rather than fear or avoid it.

Further, all too many instructors seem stuck up at the front of the classroom, almost like wooden stick figures. Some hide behind their desks and lecterns, begging for student attention or, conversely, demanding attention from the class. That physical arrangement makes discussion flow very constrained, more like a band trying to follow the baton of a hapless conductor than what needs to occur in a civil society engaged in dialogue. Teachers must learn better body language: move around the room, speak from the sides and rear of the class at times, sit on a desk—your own or a vacant one—glance around for facial clues, and continue to puzzle— "How can this be?" "What if this or that happened?" "How could we better put it together?" "Supposing…?"—the last perhaps the most important word in inquiry-discussion.

Eye 1:1 is a difficult habit for teachers to break.. In training sessions, I have come to realize that teacher resistance to change from that fixated eye habit is a psychological barrier. Some teachers simply don't want to let go of tight control of the class or of their perception of themselves as hurlers of facts and sole repository of knowledge in their classroom. Others are hamstrung by carrying the rules of deferential and polite conversation into the classroom, acting as if the discussants were waiting in line to receive a personal message. The cost in terms of lost interaction and lost opportunity to explore ideas is immeasurable; one result is actual reinforcement of student passivity and apathy. The loss to readiness for public dialogue in a free society is greater still.

Yet, all is not lost, for teachers can and do change. Ineffective eye contact and body language are learned behaviors, and what has been learned can be unlearned, although not without a willingness to face the causes of much student passivity and to struggle against old habits.

Case-study training sessions can be carefully aimed at breaking both the eye-fixation pattern and the problem of frozen body-language. Because case-study is intrinsically problem-oriented, it has the virtue of easily motivating, indeed provoking, participation. Under the wing of a trained discussion-training leader, participants practice eye control and movement followed by critique sessions to further build self-awareness. This training needs to be made a key part of teacher training and in-service programs. The result will be a more productive and varied approach to teaching, with a strong pattern of 1: all.

> **"Read not to contradict and confute;**
> **Nor to believe and take for granted,**
> **Nor to find talk and discourse:**
> **But to weigh and consider.**
>
> —Francis Bacon

7

Levels of Questioning: Definitional Problems and Values

An over-focus on the repetition of facts leads teachers away from the kinds of questions that are most productive of learning and critical thinking. Not only do fact-recall questions make for a boring exercise and one often fraught with frustration and intimidation, but the net result is much less productive of remembering than teachers are want to admit. True, the best students will prove strong at repetition and lesson-learning, but there is no necessary connection between repetition and being able to analyze a problem. The Japanese system of education, which is an extreme case of focus on memorization and recall and classroom-group drill and examination, has recently come under severe criticism by Japanese educators and scientists, among others, for its mind-dulling ways and its stress on consensus over creativity. American education, with all its many flaws, has nonetheless produced more Nobel Prize winners than most of the rest of the world combined! This is no reason for complacency, especially given growing evidence of laxity and continuing turmoil affecting American public education, but it does give grounds for distrust of simplistic solutions based on memorization and copying the Japanese; also it gives grounds for hope that sensible reform will keep open the doors of opportunity for all children. So long as the discussion process is functioning, so long as flexibility and creativity remain operational values, there is realistic hope that the American educational process can stay self-correcting.

What needs to be better defined for teachers is the nature of the questioning process. I'd like to begin with a simple axiom: A reasonable answer to an important question is of far greater significance and utility to learning than an exact answer to an unimportant question. "What did Columbus hope to prove by sailing to the New World?", is a far more important question than "What are the names of the three ships that sailed with Columbus?" Similarly, "How might an architect utilize tree-planting to reduce energy consumption in a planned new apartment building?" aids and reveals a student's thinking ability far more than "What three trees are commonly planted near apartment buildings?" It is not that the latter questions are completely unimportant; it is simply that as isolated bits of information they lead nowhere. They are dead-ended insofar as discussion goes and they do not fuel a discovery process. Yet, having observed countless teacher-led discussions and having read many examinations and quizzes given to students, I would venture to say that just such simplistic humdrum makes up a major portion of classroom testing and is the normal or accepted patter of recitation and teacher-led drill. This dulling routine fits well into the current fashion for "objective testing" (so-called)—a subject to which we will return in good time. The drill is indicative of the failure of classroom teachers to recognize that meaningful discussion and an inquiry process of education calls for a very different approach and perspective—and that you can't get critical thinking blood out of drilled turnips!

By shifting the level of questioning and tone, learning could be made far more productive of thinking. At base, we can throw around some questions of fact. Moving more toward a problem or inquiry perspective, we can move discussion forward (upward—I like to think) by asking for comparisons and contrasts. The full measure of productive thinking is achieved when we examine questions of meaning and significance, the third and highest level of teaching art. Let's take an example. At base, we can ask the students what the medieval church believed about the movements of the heavenly bodies? The students come to answer—if they have read the lesson material—that the church believed that the Earth was the center of the universe and that the sun and the stars and planets revolved around this center. After all, some learners might add, God had picked this earth as the center of his creation and it was plain to the eye to see that it was so. Having established this fact about the belief system of the medieval church, the discussion leader ups the ante by asking for a comparison. "Well, what did Galileo see through his telescope that differed with the accepted wisdom of his day?" This question can, of course, take different forms (e.g.: How did Galileo's findings conflict with the long accepted view of the planetary system? Or: How would you compare Galileo's view of the universe with that of the medieval church?)

In both of the above questions, a factual explanation is sought that details the contrast in views. I favor the idea of having students visualize looking through a telescope because it stimulates imaginative thinking. Then by defining the two contrasting views of the universe, they have a better chance of making the learning stick. Comparison and contrast always adds a glue to factual learning.

Even to this point, however, the students are still lacking the kind of catalyst that yields full critical thinking. We can assume by now that they retain the contrasting view, but do they know its significance? We can find out by asking a seemingly innocent question, one that many teachers would simply not think to ask: "What on earth did the church have to lose by allowing Galileo to expound his beliefs?" By facing this question, we can move the discussion to its highest level, raising all kinds of important value questions about freedom of inquiry and the meaning of such terms as faith, reason, clear and present danger, and a free marketplace.

Thus, simply by changing the level of questioning from fact-orientation at base to comparison/contrast at level two, and then to full problem-orientation at level three, the discussion leader can turn a boring drill into a provocative inquiry. My experience is that the students will remember far more from a zesty discovery lesson than from a well-ordered drill. More important, they will learn how to inquire and analyze and discuss; their judgmental abilities will sharpen.

Indeed, students who seem to be quite slow learners in traditional recitation classes, are often simply bored and indifferent to the dullness of the drill routine. Given half a chance to think, they will come alive and gain confidence from the inquiry process. Just as old people slow down because in isolation they are not being challenged, many students are dulled by the utter lack of stimulating investigation in so many classrooms. They are left with a smattering of knowledge but little intellectual validation.

Questions of fact help frame the study of problems and issues, but the wise teacher knows that facts are the essential ground of discourse but not the sole end or goal. The creative teacher weaves questions of fact or statements of fact into a larger tapestry which includes problems of definition and value questions. The goal is to sharpen judgment and reflective thinking, and this is best accomplished by posing a variety of types of questions and avoiding limiting discourse by fixation on facts alone.

Many teachers have not stopped to think about the important differences between questions of fact, definitional problems, and questions of value. Thus, they lose the opportunity to sharpen discussion and to pursue issues to their liveliest and most productive possibilities.

To clarify the differences, let's take a simple example. Imagine that we could paint a white line around an approximate half-mile circle of forest. Our base question of fact, let us suppose, is: "How many trees stand within this forest circle?" On its face, this seems a simple matter of counting and reporting the facts. We could send out several teams with different color paint to mark each tree as it is counted and thus come up with an accurate and verified count. But even questions of fact are not always so simple. One team wants to know if very small trees, shrub size, should be counted. Another wants to count double-trunks as the equivalent of two trees. A third group wants to omit diseased trees from the total on the grounds that they will likely soon fall over and not be harvest-able. And so it goes. Of course, what we are dealing with here is a definitional problem: For purposes of the count, what exactly constitutes "a tree"? As if this were not becoming complicated enough, a wildlife biologist, a timber company executive, and a proponent of housing for the poor come along, loudly arguing over what should happen to the forest. The executive want to clear-cut all the trees so he can sell the lumber to Japan and thereby make a profit and keep his workers employed. The housing specialist also want the trees cut down, but he wants the lumber to be barred from export; by increasing the supply of lumber in the U.S., he hopes to drive the price down and so make housing more affordable to lower income families. The wildlife biologist is very angry to hear all this and takes a completely different stance. He argues for selective cutting of old-growth timber and some thinning of the crowded new growth. He stresses that massive clear-cutting of the full forest will denude the landscape and open it up to severe soil erosion and siltation of streams for miles around. Fish breeding will virtually come to a halt and the removal of undergrowth by heavy equipment working the area will compact the soil and destroy the natural habitat of birds and animals indigenous to the forest. The timber executive, however, maintains that selective cutting is too costly and cumbersome, and that wildlife have plenty of area in which to live outside the marked forest circle; besides, he agrees to replant with fast growth pines. This somewhat pleases the low income housing specialist but not the biologist, who argues for a forest of mixed species and "not another one of your damn tree farms."

What we are dealing with in this sharp exchange is a question of values. "Should we cut down and remove all the trees in the forest?" Or, put another way, "Should clear-cutting be allowed in American forests?" The words "should" or "ought" are usually, but not always, give-aways to questions of value. They are the most difficult and the most interesting of all questions, and, properly put, they are the great generators of discussion and controversy. Note that value questions go to the heart of our belief system. They are the kind of questions that test what we stand for in life and sometimes what we are ready to die for. Unlike simple questions of opinion, though they may be that too, value questions do not deal with easy choice or simple preference. We may prefer chocolate over vanilla ice cream, going to the baseball game over attendance at a track meet, and slacks over wearing a dress, but we value the right to read what we want, to speak freely, to support or not support a ban on smoking in restaurants, to give or to withhold federal aid to education etc. Note too that values rest on certain assumptions of fact, sometimes obvious and sometimes hidden even from the person expressing the value. The teen-ager who tells her parent that, "I am old enough and I have a right to read whatever I want" is resting her case (her values) on a different approach to facts of age, discretion, freedom, rights than her parent who tells her "I won't have you reading and exposing your mind to that junk so long as you are in my house." Thus value questions lead to, underscore, and highlight factual issues and definitional problems. It is easier to see now that the teacher who focuses discussion largely on fact and fact-recall has literally lost the forest for the trees. Stuck on one kind of question, he can never really get discussion moving into the very areas and levels that are essential to long run retention of information and immediate and meaningful discourse. Sad, and oh so true in so many classes right now!

One further clarification is in order with respect to definitional problems. When the learners do not understand the MEANING of a word, we are faced with a problem of vocabulary. We need to clarify and define the word in question. This is an entirely different kind of issue than that posed by differences in opinion and perspective over how a word or term should be applied in a given circumstance; it is this puzzle that forms not a question of definition (or vocabulary) but a <u>definitional problem</u>. Is the car moving 85 miles per hour on a lightly traveled freeway in the desert within the scope of "reasonable and proper" state guidelines for remote-area driving? Is wearing a black armband in protest of government action in keeping within school guidelines for "non-provocative dress?" Is a very loud sound system playing in the back of a car or pickup truck "a public nuisance?" In these cases, we know what the words mean (vocabulary is clear) but we are puzzled as to how to apply them. Such questions afford great opportunities for making questions of fact come alive. Definitional problems or questions likewise highlight values and demand a certain body of facts be put on the table: What time was it when the young man with the blaring sound system entered the residential area? Who was complaining? Were people asleep at the time? How loud was it? etc. Definitional problems and value questions stemming from even very complex issues help to clarify and bond the facts into meaningful and more easily remembered relationships. Whatever the subject specialty or the problem under study, the sharp teacher uses all three kinds of questions in class discussions and in testing: questions of fact; definitional problems; and value questions. Also, there will be some room for simple matters of preference or opinion, which constitute a kind of fourth realm. As we have explained, such questions do not lead very far and are often confused with value choices. Preferences are legitimate ways of expressing a simple view.

Facts in lists or as isolated parts are not easily stored; facts are more easily explained and recalled when associated with definitional problems and value questions, which both magnetize the facts, order them, and add spice to the learning process. Much like a dull list of facts, dull lectures and dull reading and recitation-drill have a common denominator: all four lack puzzle, conflict, and that catalytic zest that characterizes the process of discovery and invention. Back-to-basics workbooks and drill well illustrate the point. Studies in the classroom and teacher complaints have revealed back-to-basics as a mechanical and shoddy path and a stultifying routine that has long dominated traditional education. It is really more of the same routine, however touted as innovative and a return to "real education."

In contrast to "basic education", the process of problem-centered and inquiry-based teaching and learning is alive and effective. It is kept vital by the romance and excitement of problems and issues presented in a realistic way. If you don't believe the difference between the two approaches matters all that much, try getting excited about reading a telephone book, or, for that matter, most of the textbooks on the market today.

Shortly, we will test ourselves for our understanding of the differences between the four kinds of questions discussed above: fact; definitional problems; value questions; and simple matters of opinion. But first, let's practice with a short, provocative article:

Wilderness in Silence

"Who loves the mountains leaves the flowers." Every Swiss mountain train used to carry this caution. Perhaps they still do. The slogan stuck with me over 30 years because of its simple truth: Take wildness where it is, and leave it be!

Summer! People are once again flocking to the wild lands. From every city and town, in motor homes, campers, automobiles and motorcycles come hordes of urbanites seeking, supposedly, peace and tranquility. In mountain realms, John Muir advised, "troubles fall off like autumn leaves."

Yes, it is the call of the wild. Or it was until the wildness in us became civilized. Now throbs within us a contrary beat, a thirst for all the claptrap of city living, plus the chatter and nervous background that we have grown to feed upon. The fear of quiet and the realization of our own puniness before nature is hard to face. Rather than leave the wild lands be, we insist on "civilizing" them.

Urbanites press to bring ever more roads and city comforts to the great parks and forests. Few simple camps are left, and some national parks look like mall parking lots. A pattern of preening and loud display develops: Motorcycles roar into campgrounds; tourist stores with milling crowds abound; tires crunch on gravel as motor-homes maneuver; card-games and TV erupt. Drowned out or lost are the night sounds, the wind rustling leaves, the mystery of the stars…stillness. The human voice babbles on, erasing the hoot of the owl, the soothing melody of the distant brook. Quiet is then an aberration, and nature is even viewed as "un-natural."

Thus despoiled is the sanctuary we profess to seek—an escape from the frantic life we lead in our cities. Will wilderness become extinct and the wilderness spirit along with it? Not if we can learn to look at visitation to the wild places as a special game with rules we must learn and steadfastly obey as we do with all other kinds of sport. The basic rule of the "wilderness game" is one of nature's predominance. By simple definition, a human visitor to the earth's wild places is but a bird of passage. The entry requirement is a promise to leave nothing more than footprints—a cushioned and quiet experience. Getting back to nature is not a license to play savage, certainly not with noisy modern equipment.

The wilderness game is surely different from more familiar sports: no point score or time barrier, no start and finish lines, no leagues and cheering fans, and no TV payoff. But like other sports, the game of wilderness shares a common need for rules of order to prevent disruption and commotion on the playing field. While not formalized in a rulebook, they exist as common sense boundaries we can easily recognize. These essential ground rules are trampled upon when forest and parkland become an arena for whirlwind tours and carnival theatre. Actions that smother the quiet call of the wild lands are destructive to plant and animal communities and intrude upon the privacy rights of human visitors.

Consider the effect of disrespect for rules on popular games: Spectators would wander at will onto the field of play. A player could claim a "right" to bat with an oar, another to hit a tennis ball under the net. Loud radios could be used to hassle players at matches. Beer cans would litter the fairways and laundry would hang from clubhouse windows. And greens-flags might be convenient for target practice.

Such intolerable and ludicrous situations would soon end with the appearance of rules-enforcers—umpires, police, the players themselves. To continue play, we would have to agree that the rules are inviolable.

Note, none of this obedience is "natural." It is carefully taught in school and on the field, and is the hidden price of entry to the game. We are justifiably annoyed at people who do not care about or don't try to understand the rules. We insist they learn.

The wilderness game is really no different. The need for quiet, the rule of allowing nature to predominate over human activity must be taught in every school and park. It won't be easy!

Recreational sports today are increasingly aggressive and aggression-producing, leading to a swaggering spectatorism. After their mid-twenties, most people dissociate themselves from active participation in games they have been relentlessly taught, and fall back into the passive status of "spectator sports fan." No wonder that yelling and preening are carried over into other fields of play, into nature's enclaves, where just the opposite goals and rules are called for. It is not surprising that obesity and heart disease abound in a population that has all but abandoned any commitment to lifelong exercise and active involvement with the wild lands.

Our wild places are a national resource, a sustaining and spiritual element in an increasingly pressured world. If they become a ground for playing-out city tensions, urban people will have broken a principal safety valve for mental health. Technologically-driven, super-stimulated urbanites, obsessed with "winning," will increasingly lack compassion and caring about legacy to future generations. They will be less and less able to differentiate between the wild lands and Disneylands and will become ever more content with climbing fake mountains and screaming their way through artificial waterfalls. They will scar the rocks and stare at the scenery for a few moments, and see little but background, amusement, and dollar value. And they will pick the wildflowers and bring them home wilted and dying like their own souls.

A caring approach to wilderness, a sustained effort to learn the beauty of quiet can work wonders for our lands and for ourselves. But can we rise to this kind of educational challenge?

◆   ◆   ◆

The article presents some interesting opportunities for practice at creating your own discussion guide. Take five or ten minutes now and write down some key questions that you would like your class or group to consider. Write some questions of and about facts. But also practice raising definitional problems and value issues. There is room, too, for a few lighter questions of preference or opinion, keeping in mind that the issues involved are serious. *Be sure to ask questions that force the reader into the shoes of the author, that cause a penetration of the article.* Try to avoid creating tangents and questions that call for one or two word answers.

Just as you are about to do, I ponder the article and write down questions to generate reflective thinking and to keep the discussion process going. These are not meant as a master list or questions better than your own. I'm sure we are bound to focus on many of the same issues.

Grow comfortable with your own autonomy, with your own problem-centeredness. Remember that there is no necessary and proper order of questions, for the discussion process takes on a life of its own. Yet, you must strive to come to terms with the author, to penetrate the article before deciding on what you agree or disagree. Keep your discussants focused and only then flow with the evaluation of opinions expressed. In other words, be directive but not authoritarian.

Sample Discussion Guide: <u>Wilderness in Silence</u>

a) What is "the call of the wild?" Do city people still have it?

b) Is life in our cities as frantic as claimed?

c) How does "frantic" differ from "exciting?"

d) Urban living is often described as "pressured." What kinds of expectations and life style burden the city dweller perhaps much more than rural inhabitants?

e) We go to the wild lands to seek peace and tranquility. But why do so many visitors expect to find there all the amenities of city living?

f) Is loud display (noise-making) and preening contrary to the spirit of the wild lands? (Or is it just another example of normal animal behavior?)

g) If wilderness is to be viewed as a game or sport, how does it basically different from our more familiar kinds of popular sports?

h) Birds and mammals make their own special noises in the wild lands. Why does the author maintain that humans should be restricted to being quiet? Do plants and animals have special rights?

i) Is a code of quiet conduct for human visitors reasonable? Is it an infringement on visitation rights? (Note the definitional approach to the problem).

j) Sports rules for familiar games (baseball, tennis, football etc) are taught relentlessly both in school and on the field. Why are these games given such special preference?

k) Are combative recreational sports aggression-producing?

l) Do the major combative or competitive sports channel aggression constructively or do they boster tendencies toward loud display and public preening?

m) Is there a relationship between competitive sports for the young and withdrawal from active exercise and a growing pattern of spectatorism for those past thirty?

n) Should schools be induced to change their sports education programs to favor less combative recreation aimed at lifelong health patterns?

o) What should schools teach to emphasize lifetime health? How would this effect the curriculum and big time college and professional recruiting?

p) Has nature become but a background for amusement?

And a last thought or problem pops into mind: Modern man is technologically sophisticated. From a definitional standpoint, does that mean that humans are <u>better</u> or <u>wiser</u> than all other species of plants and animals? From the viewpoint of values, should humans exercise dominion (dominate) the natural world? Should humans be obligated to stewardship in behalf of nature and for the benefit of all future generations and the planet?

These are some of the many kinds of questions that can be raised with the reading, "Wilderness in Silence." How many questions posed here are similar to questions that you wrote down? What other issues did you find important? And did you arrive at a fair mix of questions, avoiding fixation on the fact area? The ability to mix types of questions to include values and definitionals is very important as an indicator or your "set" as a teacher and discussion leader. We need to practice regularly to widen the range of our questioning and so broaden and deepen our ability to develop critical thinking.

Facts—Definitions—Values—Opinions???

Instructions: After each of the following questions or statements on this self-test, indicate which one of the four choices is most involved: Is it a question or statement of fact, of value, a definitional problem, or a simple opinion? Explain your choice!

1) It is far more important to put tax money into health research than into more tanks and guns.

2) The question is whether the governor used informed judgment.

3) Was the young genius Einstein recognized for his abilities by his high school teachers?

4) What we are really arguing is: How many visitors a day constitutes the maximum carrying capacity of the park?

5) Older people should be given preferential rates in parking and also course credits for their life experiences.

6) As an experienced carpenter, I think I can prove that the reason the door sticks is because of the recent rains.

7) Who invented the refrigerator?

8) She looks better in a long dress than in slacks.

9) The weather satellite picture indicates that it should rain by Tuesday.

10) Golf may be a nice game, but it doesn't prove strong for aerobic conditioning.

11) How many times did Edison try filaments for his electric light bulb before he came up with a satisfactory solution?

12) Students should learn to think critically, and if they don't, their years of education have largely been wasted.

8

Critical Thinking, Discussion Leading, and Case-Study

Why can't my students think for themselves? Why are they so unprepared and so often intellectually lazy? Why do they expect me to do their thinking for them? These are common teacher plaints, sometimes even noted as major concerns in the professional literature of education. If the truth be known, relatively few teachers and professors are using the kinds of materials and the discussion strategies that would build in their students a mental set and a taste for critical thinking. Thus the classroom atmosphere and procedure dulls the possibilities for creating the very qualities of mind which educators avow as their wish and their goal.

In a massive study aimed at finding out what actually goes on in the classroom, and involving over one-thousand classroom visits in schools across the country, Goodlad found that teachers use a very restricted range of pedagogical strategies, mainly those that employ looking up answers and recall of information. There is little emphasis on the evaluation of knowledge and on intellectual curiosity, with most lessons begun and followed by giving instructions and orders and general teacher talk. The study found that in an average day at senior high school, teachers talked over 90 percent of the time open for discussion. Essentially left as passive and often bored spectators, with little fostering of the ability to think rationally and evaluate knowledge, the students turn off and simply go through the motions necessary to complete the course. At the college level, conditions are much the same or worse. Professor talk dominates the classroom hours.

Part of the problem for education lies within the larger American society, which has long placed too great an emphasis on the quizmaster mentality (shooting back the correct answer to minutely factual questions, as is typically seen on television game shows—as if that were indeed a true measure of wisdom). Even more disturbing is the pressure to conform and to shy away from critical thinking because we think it is somehow not polite or "nice" (i.e.: non-controversial). Americans commonly confuse the word "critical" with negativism—even with lack of patriotism—conveniently missing the point that the opposite of critical thinking is "uncritical thinking"—which is not even thinking! Uncritical "thinking" may sound polite, but it can only lead to technological and policy blunders that all too often are featured in the news.

One does not have to spend long years in school or university to learn to run with the herd or spout silly ideas. Such "thinking" is more properly characterized as "bull" and is perhaps a convenient way to pass time. Education, as an Oxford Don once commented to an entering class, is a thoughtful process geared to producing a graduate "who can instantly recognize when a man is talking rot!"

In thinking "critically," we seek to penetrate to the core, taking a fully open or "no holds barred" look at a problem or issue. Our guiding principle is candor—objectivity toward the evidence and honesty toward all. We go where our rational mind leads us, while also staying respectful of the intuitive and the hunch, as well as those with differing ideas and opinions.

Even the term "critical thinking" leaves some latitude for your own imagination. It is not a case of copying down my own definition or that of some other expert or observer. Rather, it is a case of wrestling with the two words: critical and thinking. As we have noted, these have little to do with loose talk or "bull." Critical thinking, by contrast, certainly includes the following activities, but not necessarily all at once or in any order of priority:

> # an ability to raise important questions and explore alternatives;

> # a keen sense of what is missing or needed to solve a problem;

> # an ability to deal with complexity and to hypothesize;

> # a sensitivity that draws in the background environment of an issue;

> # a knack for separating important facts from material that is peripheral or less important;

> # a healthy skepticism, and a corresponding ability and willingness to test one's theories and explore one's feelings;

> # a willingness to challenge and be challenged;

> # an ear to what others are saying and an ability to step into another person's shoes.

Obviously, every person, educated or not, is capable of some, if not most of these functions and capabilities. It is a matter of degree and often of time and circumstance. The above list is not meant to be all-inclusive, but mainly exemplary. Candor leads us to see when we are thinking critically and when we are not. And here too, even the experts trap themselves in wishful thinking.

The tendency to submerge the critical capacity and to go along with the prevailing "wisdom," was long ago noted by the great French observer of American society, Alexis de Tocqueville. In 1835, commenting on the pressures for conformity that inhere is democratic societies and that seemed to him to threaten the debasement of the character of its citizens, he remarked in a long famous passage:

> In that immense crowd which throngs the avenues to power in the United States, I found very few men who displayed any of that manly candor and that masculine independence of opinion which frequently distinguished the Americans in former times, and which constitutes the leading feature in distinguished characters, wheresoever they may be found. It seems, at first sight, as if all the minds of the Americans were formed upon one model, so accurately do they correspond in their manner of judging. A foreigner does, indeed, sometimes meet with Americans who dissent from these vigorous formularies; with men who deplore the defects of the laws, the mutability and the ignorance of democracy; who even go so far as to observe the evil tendencies which impair the national character, and to point out such remedies as it might be possible to apply; but no one is there to hear these things besides yourself, and you, to whom these secret reflections are confided, are a foreigner and a bird of passage. They are very ready to communicate truths which are useless to you, but they continue to hold a different language in public.

Part of the greater lesson of history is that honest men and women can and will differ over the meaning and importance of facts, events, and ideas. The great lesson of democracy is that they should work out their differences in the open marketplace of ideas. To withdraw from the rigors of that marketplace, to play the game of going along just to get along, or to play ignorant and put on a pleasant face, is to surrender in whole or part the legacy and the responsibility of freedom.

Some educators and parents have tried to avoid the dilemma posed by critical thinking and controversy by creating a special area of curriculum called, "controversial issues"—as though these could be isolated and handled gingerly in a guarded and sanitized arena. Quite frankly this is educational nonsense, for controversial issues—so called, are not only an inherent part of any vital curriculum, but more often than not are its very heart and soul. Those issues reflect the most important values of society and the essential currents of change. Indeed, they are the issues that make the curriculum come alive and are the most relevant to citizens and students. Just as there cannot be a chemistry without chemicals, there cannot be a larger curriculum without the great issues. That some chemicals are complex or unstable does not make them "controversial" but does make them deeply interesting. Whatever the course of study, in science, social science or the humanities, it is the differences in viewpoint and the contrast of views (the very instability) that offers the most fertile ground for discussion and for learning the facts and how to think critically about problems.

And herein lies one of the greatest strengths of case-study, for the problem-posing cases easily and naturally form the ground or arena for the kind of intensive analysis and discussion that generates critical thinking, heightened interest, and joyful learning for both student and teacher. We'll look more deeply at case-study after some thoughts on strategy for discussion-leading:

Some Prickly Thoughts on Discussion-Leading

Discussion leading is a fine and difficult art. Many teachers would rather hear themselves talk than listen to the awakening of critical thinking in their students. This is a psychological as well as a pedagogical problem, for if the class is to come alive the discussion leader must be aware that his listening skills are critical.

Discussion leading calls for sharp ability at ASKING QUESIONS and stimulating dialogue via an inquiring attitude. It is a path different from both debate and lecture. Your job as a leader is not to figure out the problem for the class or to tell people what the author of the case or reading had to say. Your job is to help the class to figure these things out for themselves. Think of yourself not as the fountainhead of information, nor as a quizmaster trying to trick people or find minor items to test. Rather, see yourself as a gadfly trying to guide the learners (including yourself) into properly defining the issues and problems and then helping them to move on toward a judgment or solution based on the facts and issues at hand.

People reading the exact same material come up with incredibly different facts and interpretations. This should come as no surprise. As previously noted in an earlier chapter, courtroom juries go through the very same process in arriving at judgments about both evidence (facts) and guilt or innocence. Therefore, you the leader, must put yourself in the author's shoes, making sure the learners are agreed on the facts as presented: What was actually said? What does it mean? How does it relate—and is it valid?—these are the 3 prime inquiries and in order of priority. No one (and especially the leader) should be criticizing the case-story or the article on the table until all present are agreed upon what was said and what it means (both of these points may of themselves stir up a goodly amount of probing and discussion.) Through all this process, remember the famous dictum of Coleridge that honest inquiry demands "a willing suspension of disbelief."

In the words of Francis Bacon: "Read not to contradict and confute; nor to believe and take for granted; nor to find talk and discourse: <u>but to weigh and consider</u>."

One need not read or know much of anything to participate in a bull-session. In contrast, genuine discussion calls for careful reading and a willingness to think carefully and be candid. This goes for both the discussion leader and the participants or discussants. No room for grandstanding and ego trips here, no great lectures and claims of privilege. The arena of discussion or forum is a true open marketplace of ideas within the limits of the subject and reading scheduled. The leader will have formulated a short list of key questions aimed at stimulating the dialogue, and initially targeted at defining the exact issues and problems of that day. Simple questions related to a particular phrase or thought in the case often help greatly to clarify. By contrast, long, complicated questions or those which call only for a yes-or-no answer either cause confusion or dampen discussion. For example, using a reading from the urban scene, the discussion leader might open by asking: "What does Mumford mean when he speaks of the megamachine? (This forces participants into the reading.) Then after some discussion and clarification by the class, the leader might probe some more: "Well, how does he see the mentality of the megamachine affecting urban development and planning?" In time the discussion leader will need to ask: "Why do you agree or disagree with Mumford?" Note that the leader must studiously avoid asking for an evaluation or solution until that point is reached where the class fully comprehends the problem. A sharp discussion leader never falls into the dead-end of asking for opinions or judgment as an opener, for that is sure to dampen the case, allow much misinformation to circulate, and induce learner laziness at preparation.

So keep the discussion on course and lively. Politely but firmly avoid tangents that threaten to throw the dialogue into a bull session, where everyone simply talks off the top of the head. Know the value of keeping quiet and waiting for learners to mull a question. Know too that a good question does not have to be explained. It rides and entices under its own power. Indeed the temptation to explain questions means one of two things: the question itself is too complicated or confusing; or the discussion leader doesn't understand the importance of wait-time, or is tempted to fall back into the bad habit of lecturing.

Of course, it is to be expected that learners will try to box a teacher or discussion leader into the traditional god-like or lecture role. "Oh, tell us the answer," they will beg. But your task is to turn the tables on learner laziness and make learning through discussion an ACTIVE, enjoyable, and productive experience which sharpens critical thinking all around. Learn to listen. Listening skills are golden. Learn to wait for other participants to jump in. Ask for clarification when required. And ask your questions in a way that encourages thinking, your own as well as the discussants. Voice tone can be quite critical. Remember too that a key goal is penetration of the material under question, and you will have to watch carefully to keep the discussion on track and well focused. To a sharp discussion leader/teacher, a reasonable answer to an important question is of greater significance than an exact answer to a question of small import.

Finally, you must encourage people to jump in by creating an atmosphere for learning that is conducive to the free exchange of ideas. Let people know how interested you are in the process of dialogue, in hearing their ideas develop. And you can always quote that great Chinese proverb:

> "Who asks a question is a fool for two minutes; who does not ask is a fool forever."

"Time is what it takes me to explain the problem and eternity is what it takes for you to understand it."

9

Case-Study: How it Aids Teaching

l) The goal of case-study is the development of superior powers of judgment through a process of active group discussion and decision-making.

2) Focus is on the analysis of actual or simulated problems and solutions, thus nurturing skill in reflective and analytical thinking—at both theoretical and practical levels.

3) The objective in case-study is not simply the organization of facts and materials and the recall and recitation of information. While such skills are components of the case-study process, they are aids to the main thrust: Using group interaction to work through a decision on how best to solve the problem posed by the case.

4) Thus, case-study is a "decisional" as opposed to a lecture or expository form of teaching and learning.

5) Case method has proven particularly efficient at exercising the ability to transfer from familiar kinds of problems or situations to novel circumstances requiring the application of similar principles.

6) By internalizing strengths in analysis and decision-making, the case-study learner develops skills that do not extinguish easily, as contrasted to what frequently occurs in more traditional learning with its dependency relationships between student and teacher.

7) Case-study strengthens critical thinking. Because it is problem-centered, facts and information actually gather and retain more easily than in traditional lesson-learning.

8) Case-study is not an educational panacea, but a very important (and under-utilized) tool for teaching and training. The case method should not be confused with problem-solving in which there is a set conclusion with little room for differences of opinion.

9) Case-study teachers and trainers must learn to guide discussion but not dominate it. They must know the value of questions and of silence or "wait-time" for student deliberation. They must respect the process of democratic dialogue and be adept at avoiding the tendency of learners to box teachers into a godlike role: "Tell us the answer."

10) Conclusions are not really understood apart from the arguments whereby they are reached! It is very difficult to absorb this very list of case study goals and operational considerations without partaking in an active process of case-analysis with a class. Re-read these ten pointers after you have hands-on experience with the case process and you will see how much more meaningful they become.

And now, on to some real case-studies…

The following practice cases are fictional, although based on real-life happenings. Any resemblance of the characters to persons living or dead is purely coincidental.

Instruction: Carefully penetrate each of the cases so that everyone participating is agreed first on the nature of the problem and what exactly the contending parties are saying and claiming. Don't take things for granted just because the case is printed and read. People interpret facts and statements in many ways and often forget key elements, or read things in from their own frame of reference.

Have the participants clarify the situation in their own words and get a balance of views on the table, giving a fair hearing to all sides. Discover if anything is missing in the way of argument or facts, but don't try to create additional problems or other examples that might obscure, lose, or confuse the issues in this particular case. It's o.k. to make a few assumptions or suppositions for the sake of sharpening discussion or getting around a snag, but stay within the general bounds of the case or tangents will form and attention will wander from the problem at hand.

Practicing with the first few cases, it is of primary importance to learn how to focus and to exchange views candidly but respectfully toward the opinions of others. When and if discussion does begin to wander away from the case, pull it back with a request for summation or a question that demands penetration of the issues and facts of the case.

As a general rule, discussion should begin with the nature of the problem, with what actually happened or was said or claimed. Case discussion should not open with focus on the outcome or with what participants feel is good or bad about the case. Again, learn to focus on the stage and players as given in the case-study. Then discussion should broaden to meanings and definitional questions and arguments that help clarify the issues. Only after these clarifications are made and participants fully grasp the issues and are agreed on the positions of the contending parties should full focus fall on the question of right and wrong and a just and workable solution.

Too frequently teachers focus quickly on the decision rather than on the facts and arguments. This undercuts the thinking process and often ruins the case as a tool for sharpening critical thinking skills. A good discussion takes careful preparation and careful thought. The process of discovery takes time. So learn to labor and to wait.

Order of cases:

1) Classroom Management and Discipline

2) Admissions Policy for the Freshman Class

3) The Shrinking Safety Net

4) Junk Food/Junk Education

5) Culture Shock and Immigration Policy

Introduction to Case #1: On Classroom Management

It is time to look at classroom management as a function of sharp organization and direction rather than mainly a question of bad behavior or discipline. Classroom control or lack of it is partly a matter of "presence"—something allied to personality and even charisma. We have all seen examples of physically large teachers with deep voices who cannot even come close to the smooth management of a classroom run by someone half their size. Of course, we have seen the opposite as well. Why is it that one teacher seems to almost automatically convey a sense of purposeful work and a peaceful classroom atmosphere, while another virtually foments confusion and disorder? Why is it that one professor puts everyone to sleep, while another inspires questioning, probing, mental alertness and interest in the subject matter? There are no easy answers to such questions in terms of personality, but it is fairly safe to assume that good planning and a problem-centered work atmosphere channels energy constructively and does not allow it to take negative and aberrant forms. Unfortunately, we can't teach charisma.

Herein we will view management in terms of problem-oriented teaching goals as well as "control issues." We'll see the strengthening value of good questioning technique, particularly in the realm of definitional problems and values. We'll learn a bit about how to motivate interest and get students involved as perhaps the most effective way to avoid discipline/apathy problems to begin with. Apathy and withdrawal are not usually seen as a problem, for the teacher is not distracted or bothered unless he chooses to be, but it is really the other side of the coin of aversion to learning. Indeed, it may be the worst offender in terms of teaching learners how NOT to learn. As psychological counselors are want to say, indifference is even worse than hostility. In expressing anger, at least the problem is brought to the surface and the "other party" is recognized rather than ignored and negated.

In problem-centered teaching, the withdrawn learner (or teacher)—the one who won't participate in a discussion process—is viewed as just as much a problem as is the student who is loud and pushy. Both types of learner-personalities are hostile or unhelpful to the democratic process of free inquiry and a marketplace of opinion. And what of the teacher who hides behind his or her lecture notes or drowns the class in constant make-work assignments? Think about that!

Thus, in case-study and other problem-oriented teaching, we are much concerned with increasing motivation and working through the problem on the table. We are less frantic about minor noise in the classroom. So long as the main focus is on the work at hand and constructive effort is underway, the students are attentive and respectful to each other and to the questions and ideas under consideration, so long can we delight in the assurance that critical thinking is being honed. The process of inquiry sets the tone for discipline and for disciplined thinking, with the teacher serving as guide rather than drillmaster. It's not an easily learned art like driving a car, but is more like the tentative feel of mountain climbing or the synchronized effort at choral music or water ballet.

As you proceed to the next case-study concerning discipline, remember to listen well to both sides. Carefully penetrate the case-story so there is at least class agreement on the nature of the problem and on what exactly the contending parties are saying. Discover if anything is missing by way of fact or argument, but don't stretch things too far. It's o.k. to make reasonable assumptions if that will help clarify the issues.

This is the time to write your own discussion questions for case # 1, and the remaining cases as well, before comparing them to those accompanying the story. Your own input and perspective is very important in terms of sharpening your ability to write questions and penetrate the issues of the case. While your own approach will doubtless strike similar chords to mine, it need not necessarily take the same order or form. The final test of the worth of a question may even be in how it is asked and in the wait-time that you give students to answer.

1. "Bad Chemistry," Bad Manners, and/or Bad Teaching

When Arel Seradda entered the office of Vice Principal Dan Ossif, it was evident that he was hardly cowed by the charge of disrespectful and abusive behavior lodged against him by his economics and math teacher. A blue sweater slung over his shoulder, he glided into the room with a sporty wave that tried to mask his frown of concern, and nodded a tentative, "Good morning, Mr. Ossif,...I guess I'm in trouble, no?" Ossif didn't answer, but pointed to a chair and turned to finish some routine business before spinning around again to face his charge. "O.K. Arel, this time you've gone too far. I thought you agreed to control yourself in Mr. Bermatta's class, to do the required work quietly and without complaint and to keep your thoughts about teaching to yourself. That was our agreement last time, was it not? And now you face suspension and possible transfer to another school."

"Transfer and suspension? Wow! I didn't do anything that bad. I made two out-loud remarks about the crummy work assignments and he throws me out of his room. It was no big deal. Everyone knows that he gives us this constant busy work just so he won't have to teach. That guy...."

"Now wait a minute," Ossif broke in, "Mr. Bermatta is not on trial here. You are in this office because you not only broke his rules of classroom decorum and procedure, but your outbursts subject him to ridicule and break down class respect for the teacher. No teacher has to put up with that. Further, Arel, you broke our agreement made just two months ago. Remember, I promised to get you into the honors creative writing class next semester if you would do your best in math-econ and behave yourself in a class that we both recognize just does not fit your style. I tried to be adaptable; you did not. What you have to learn is that there are all kinds of people in this world, and they may have very different approaches to teaching. One of the big lessons in life is that we have to be adaptable...flexible. It would be a dull world if we were all the same..."

"Mr. Ossif, I hear what you are saying and I appreciate your need to defend Mr. Bermatta because you are both part of the system. But we both know what educational reformers are saying about the lack of imaginative teaching in America's schools. That class could be a model for what is wrong with American education. First thing we arrive, we have to copy every day from the blackboard, an endless outline which everyone knows he copies from an old notebook that Mr. Bermatta doubtless put together twenty years ago. The examples are not current. That copy work eats up fifteen minutes every day except Friday when we get a test on outline terms and formulas. If he would simply xerox the darn thing, it would free up time for class discussion and we might all have to do some thinking. But no, we are told the outline is a way of learning accuracy, patience, and discipline. Then we read from the textbook and answer questions, which is just another way of copying. Do we discuss the problems we find? Hardly. He tells us his view and is not responsive to other perspectives. And should class discussion become intense, he claims that we are becoming unruly. And out come the worksheets. There are few problems for analysis, no hypothesis to test, no experiments…nothing. We might as well be in a gulag. And he's not even interested in the kids, and sits reading the stock market or the real estate section just as soon as he sees the class is pinned down in copywork. The class is not just dull, it's insufferable! And if I have the guts to cry out that the work is flat, empty, totally boring…I should not be treated as some kind of slave or troublemaker. This is supposed to be a school in a free country, not a prison…."

"Arel, let's hold it there. You've had your say and you said it all before. It doesn't change the fact of your headstrong misbehavior and inflexibility. And what you leave out is that many students fully accept Mr. Bermatta's classes and find his structured work assignments are quite fair and a solid way of earning a grade. Not everyone is into deep thinking and fancy lessons. That causes a lot of insecurity for many students, and frankly, for many teachers and parents. You should feel fortunate that you are learning that life is varied and that work is not all a bed of roses."

"Sure. Copy, copy, copy. A great educational scam for producing robots, but hardly the kind of learning needed in a democracy. Now take Mrs. Julian's class, by contrast."

"Let's just leave other teachers out of this, Arel. I've explained to you a dozen times that we are all different, both students and teachers. We have to learn to live with those differences and to appreciate that that's what makes the world go round. You cannot set yourself up as the arbiter of what is right and what is wrong in education and life."

"But Mr. Ossif, that cuts both ways. I'm already being set up as a scapegoat by arbiters who are telling me that to get along I have to go along. If I apply what I learned in history class to this situation, I might conclude that we are no longer interested in developing a school system that nourishes creative thinking. Maybe that's the reason we are sliding downhill as a nation? And if you think that I am strong on this point, you should hear my father!"

Mr. Ossif paused for a number of seconds. He took some deep, quiet breaths and shut his eyes. He wished he had transferred Arel to a different teacher months ago, but now there was little time left in the semester. Such bad chemistry: Arel Serrada and Mr. Bermatta. This headstrong but bright young man. And a teacher who is admittedly not at all innovative, but who has served the district well for sixteen years. Yes, he was probably dull as hell, but that is hardly an unusual situation. Maybe the district could contract for some in-service, and people like Bermatta could get a chance to refuel and see some creative teachers at work. Oh well, that is another question. The behavior problem is what's on the table. Got to talk to those parents and get this kid straightened out…. Mr. Ossif stood up and paced. His hand jabbed in a kind of warning.

"So, Serrada, there you go on the attack again. Don't you see yourself as doing anything wrong? Nothing?"

"I admit that I'm part of the problem. But, I'm responding to a larger problem that administrators don't seem to want to handle. O.k., sure, I admit that I sounded off when I should have bit my lip. My lips are bleeding from a semester of frustration. Recently, I read an essay in English class on Frank Lloyd Wright, the architect. He said that if he had to choose, he'd take honest arrogance over hypocritical humility. I guess I took the lesson to heart. I can promise to try for better self-control but I feel like I am suffocating in that class. I need air.

"Yuh, air, lots of air. Mostly hot air. Your glands are working overtime, Arel. You're a well-meaning sophomore—a wise fool. And you are painting us both into a corner. I won't have that. And the school system can't live with prima donnas, however just they may think their cause. You've become a thorn in the side to one of our faculty. And I can't trust you to toe the line. I'm afraid we'll have to have your parents up in my office tomorrow. And depending on Mr. Beratta's willingness to take you back, you may well find yourself dropped from the class, suspended, or even transferred to another school. Let me be clear about that. The law gives us that right. We have 2800 young people to care for here and we can't run an open shop for every dissident, for every whim and fancy. At this school, the line is drawn at rude and offensive behavior, whatever the reason—real or imagined. You better think about that, and, if you are lucky, about what you might say by way of apology to both Mr. Bermatta and the class. Now you wait in the outer office until the end of the day and I'll be in contact with your parents for a conference tomorrow morning."

Discussion:

1) Imagine that you were characterizing Arel Seradda to a social worker or school counselor. How would you describe him? Would your characteriza-

tion change if you were introducing him to a college admissions officer?—to a group of parents attending a political rally?

2) Is Mr. Ossif, the vice-principal, being more understanding or officious?

3) What is the best way for a teacher to deal with a student such as Arel?

4) Is this a case of "bad chemistry" between teacher and student? What exactly does that term imply?

5) Is Mr. Bermatta's teaching style within the norm of "good teaching"? If not, is it too late for him to change? And what kind of changes would you recommend?

6) Must a vice principal necessarily back a teacher whose only major fault, if it be one, is dullness? Is the teacher in this case as described "burnt out"? And what accounts for the fact that many students fully accept his style of teaching?

7) Does Arel Seradda know something about the educational system that the system is reluctant to face? Would Arel be better off in a private school? Is he an inflexible and delinquent student?

8) Would the public schools be better off without the Arel Seraddas of this world? Or would it be better to get rid of the teachers like Mr. Bermatta?

9) The vice principal mused over the benefit of more teacher in-service training as a way of energizing instruction. Would this help, and how would it work? Why is it so late in coming?

10) What would be the best possible outcome of the parent conference set up by Mr. Ossif?

11) Should Arel have been transferred out of his math-econ class long before things came to this impasse? Whose fault was it that he was programmed into Mr. Bermatta's class in the first place? Would a sharp counseling system have avoided this kind of clash by preventative action? What would that entail?

12) Has the vice principal played his role well? Did he have any other alternative?

13) Is learning <u>adaptability</u> one of the main goals of education? Does this include adaptability to whatever the teacher demands or fails to demand of

the students? And how would this "going along" in order to learn discipline differ from army training?

14) Is one of the main goals of education learning to think and speak for oneself—learning to reject conformity for the sake of conformity? How does this square with the learning of adaptability?

15) Could Arel have made his point in a less offensive way? How?

16) Is American education suffering because of its continuing acceptance of busy-work and unimaginative teaching?

2. Admissions Policy for the Freshman Class

When the seniors at highly academic Alcatan High School meet in The Corner Coffee Shop, the talk inevitably turns to hopes for college acceptance. Over eighty-five percent of Alcatan seniors go on to higher education, including a large share to prestigious institutions. In recent years, their hopes for a first choice invitation to top or "flagship" universities and colleges have been dimmed by admission policies which place priority on obtaining a heterogeneous student body-one that shows ethnic, racial, geographical, socio-economic, gender, and cultural diversity. In seeking a freshman class today, the top public and many private universities try to meet the requirements of civil rights law and public financing by balancing various factors in combination with traditional standards of good grades and test scores. High grades alone are not a guarantee of formal acceptance, especially at flagship schools thought most desirable choices by students and their parents.

In some states with large minority populations, it is a very contentious issue. And in a few states with huge systems of publicly financed higher education, the standards for college acceptance have given rise to a discontented public. For example, California draws one fourth of all the world's immigrants, and population pressure there has made it impossible for the campuses of first choice to accommodate all the thousands of eligible students; most of these go on to institutions of second or third choice, at least for the first few years.

The flagship schools, with the big names and the best academic reputations, are the centers of greatest contention. Each can easily draw over 20,000 applications for only about 4000 freshman spaces. And in some examples across the country, more than 6,500 of the applicants to a single flagship campus have straight-A high school grades. Thus, even without the pressure of civil rights mandates and affirmative action guidelines, several thousand students would be turned away each year at top choice schools.

Greg Baterman, a top student at Alcatan, could barely contain his frustration and anger over the letter of rejection he received one Saturday in February. He had long looked forward to attending Barnelle. And he had worked especially hard that year at tough courses, while bringing his grade point average up to a 3.8. As editor of the Alcatan student newspaper and a letterman in track and field, he was fairly confident that he would make second or third pick. But such was not to be, and he would have to be satisfied with one of several universities that he had applied to as a backup. Hands thrust in his pockets, a look of some despair on his face, he wandered into the Corner Coffee Shop, where some of his friends and acquaintances were gabbing over desert. "Hey Greg, you're awfully quiet today. What's eating you?" someone asked.

"Well, I'm not going to Barnelle," he replied, throwing the letter of non-acceptance on the table. Asphalt State, same thing.

"Nor me either," intoned Joan Nobel. "I got shafted! They say that there just is not enough room for all the many fine applicants, and that the university has to give priority to obtaining a diverse freshman class. Can you imagine that?—I thought I am very diverse."

"They said diverse, not perverse, Joan," Rickey Tallin joked.

"We'll ignore that," she continued. "The problem is partly timing. If we were born ten years earlier, not a person here would have any difficulty getting into a first choice school. The private universities have become so expensive that many seniors are choosing the better public universities. And then there is the matter of affirmative action."

"Right. And there is an unfairness there. Why are we being made to bear the burden of past discrimination and economic failings? It's not my fault that my father worked his way out of poverty and got a good education and a well-paying job. Why should somebody get extra attention and favor from college admissions because they are poor or belong to some ethnic group? I'm willing to compete one on one, but I don't think it right morally or legally to be handicapped."

"Now, hold it, Greg," chimed in Ezra Hamilton. You run track with me and you know that the man on the outside lane starts from a more advanced position than somebody on the inside. That's because he has a longer way to run. And a kid from the ghetto or an immigrant student, say, already has the cards stacked against him in terms of language and economic support. Sure there are exceptions. But by and large they don't start the race to college on the same line as you and me. Since they have more to overcome to begin with, I think it's only fair that they be given some special consideration."

"But college is different from a track meet," Greg responded. The whole purpose of college is intellectual advancement, and entrance should be almost wholly dictated by proof of intellectual power. I know there should be a few exceptions, like for athletes, say, or people who have a special musical or artistic talent...but not as a general rule."

"Depends whose ox is gored," Jaime Sanchez opined. The question is where do you draw the line. A public university, say Barnelle or Michigan, can't stay a hangout for rich Anglos—or for any group for that matter. The campus has to represent the larger community in all its diversity if it is to serve all the public. Rich and poor, Asian and white, male and female, all the geographical areas have to be fairly represented if they are to be fairly served. We should not end up training doctors, for example, that end up mainly in the cities and in the richer areas at that. Besides, a college education is not simply an intellectual experience. It's a full life experience of meeting people with different opinions and different backgrounds and exchanging ideas and growing. We should not be training an elite to run a feudal society. The university must train people to confront the very issues that are so important to the future of our state and the country."

"Hold it," Rickey Tallin came in on a more serious note. What is more important than intellectual development, Jaime? A university is not a department store or a bank. There you can make the case for equality of opportunity much better. By its very nature a university is an elite institution, catering to mind power. If you don't think so, why have any minimum standard at all? For example, the Master Plan for education in California says the UC system is open to the top 12 percent or so of high school seniors—or now the best students from every high school. They don't have open enrollments because they have an intellectual standard—and they shouldn't let it be eroded, however many students are claimed to be in the top group of applicants."

"Wait a minute," Jaime shot back, "the university is not easing anything. Everyone admitted, save perhaps some athletes and special talented applicants, is already in the top academic group of eligibles as mandated by the California Master Plan. What they are doing is giving some advantage to top high school students who are under-represented in the student body. Blacks and Hispanics make up a small fraction of the flagship schools, less than 8 percent, but they are about 30 percent of high school seniors.

We have to do better if all people are to have a fair chance at a top education, especially those who need to break the circle of poverty and later stand as role models. Look at it as an investment in the state's future. But also don't get me wrong: On a personal level, I sympathize with Greg and Joan. I wish they could get accepted by their first choice schools. But we have to look at the larger picture. Anyway, you can easily transfer to Barnelle or Asphalt in your junior year."

"So you are giving two rain-checks to Greg and Joan. But what about me, poor Maya Chang? We Asians, you know, are more than twice as likely to be eligible for flagship schools as whites, and more than six times as eligible as other minorities. We study hard and over one-third of us, who are seniors, are ready for the best schools. Yet, we are very under-represented at first choice institutions. That's unfair, and the rumor is that a silent quota system is working against us. At high schools like Alcatan we have very high standards. Yet our grade point average is judged on the same scale as much less academic schools. It really makes me angry..."

Ezra Hamilton chuckled. "Come off it, Maya. Asians have almost 30 percent of the freshman class and you are still complaining? I'm up to my knees in tears. You people are doing far better than those of us who have been here for generations. Asians are very fortunate to have a close family system rather than our legacy of slavery and family breakdown."

Maya pouted for a moment and then smiled. "Yes, I know and sympathize, Ezra, really. But many Asians have also been here for generations and that is not recognized. Further, I feel people have to pull themselves up by their bootstraps. Even so I also believe in government help and view education as an investment. I don't know what the answer is for sure, but quotas are simply not fair. For years they used to discriminate against Jews and others considered 'unacceptable' by the establishment."

By this time, Greg Baterman had calmed down. While he still had the bad taste of rejection, his keen mine feasted on the debate between his friends. He suddenly developed a new perspective. "I've got a solution," he announced. "Really. Let me put it on the table. I mean there is a question of fairness. What has to occur is a limitation on what I now see as a kind of arbitrary action by the university system. Now, hold a minute and let me explain. I guess I have to agree that a public university, particularly, must find a fair representation of all the various populations in the state—while at the same time keeping a high academic standard. Not everyone can get their first pick university. In listening to you here this afternoon, I've changed my thinking somewhat."

"Well, what exactly do you mean, Greg, spell it out," one of the onlookers urged.

"O.K. There is both fairness and unfairness in offering special consideration to applicants, whether because of sex, age, ethnicity, or athletic ability. Life itself is unfair. O.K.? So what I want is to make things equally unfair to all. Equally unfair means, if you think about it, equally fair. It rains on all sides of the field. So here's my plan: First, we open up the applicant pool so we increase the overall number of those eligible for the colleges caught in the enrollment squeeze. In other words, we enlarge the surplus of applicants to include a better mix of students. The university reserves 50 percent of the spaces in the freshman class strictly on the basis of highest academic performance. Now, the other 50 percent is the sticking point. Up to now, the admissions officers decide who gets how many extra points or how much weight for all the special considerations—ethnicity, poverty, gender, you name it. I want to stop them from doing that, because it is really an impossible task that leads to much unfairness. There is no way to fairly weigh these special factors against one another. So in my plan, everyone not taken in by the first round, would automatically be put into a lottery pool. Out of some 40,000 applicants to flagship schools, who aren't chosen in the first round, only the lottery would be used to pick the final 50 percent of the freshman class."

At this, everyone began talking and shouting at once.

Greg held up his hand and asked to be allowed to finish. "We'll discuss this in a minute, but first listen a bit more. I know that the lottery is also unfair because by its nature, luck becomes the king. But a lottery has the merit of ending this crazy system we have now, where we are all pitted against each other and by different standards. In a lottery, all the eligibles are equal. Every college in the country could benefit from such a system. And I want to say that I could better accept rejection by a lottery than by any other means. What do you think?"

Discussion:

1) Immigration policy is set by the federal government. Is California bearing an unfair share of the burden of educating new arrivals to the U.S.? If so, should the expenses of college education caused by "new arrivals" be paid for by the U.S. government? Should other states with less pressure for admission be required to subsidize or otherwise aid impacted states?

2) Berkeley and UCLA, Barnelle and Asphalt State, have more straight-A student-applicants than can be accommodated by the total places available in the freshman class. Assuming only straight-A students were to be admitted, how should the university make the selection? Would a lottery help?

3) How would you define "affirmative action"?

4) A diverse class representative of the mix of population in the state is the goal. Should this also be the goal of each department of the university, such as biology, chemistry, or Spanish?

5) Both high school grades and college admissions test scores (e.g. SAT) are heavily weighted in considering an applicant for admission to the university? Is a national examination system the fairest and most objective way to choose a freshman class?

6) Is the university's prime task the training of an intellectual elite? Are there other and equally important aspects of the mission of higher education?

7) By choosing a freshman class from among the highest scorers, the university might already be assuring itself of academic respectability by common standards. Would a more significant measure of its success be taken by how much <u>improvement</u> it could show given not just a class of high scorers, but a more representative group of the population?

8) Since applicants turned down by the most popular campuses can look forward to eventual transfer to these same colleges, if they do acceptable work elsewhere, is the system basically fair?

9) Greg Baterman seems to have changed his position somewhat after listening to his fellow classmates discuss the university admissions dilemma in California and elsewhere. What would account for his change of view? And how exactly did it change?

10) Would Baterman's changing perspective be evidence for the importance of a diversity of views and people in any college class?

11) Rickey Tallin feels he is being made to bear the burden for past discrimination. Yet, older adults usually feel that the younger generation is less responsible than their own. Who is right in this matter of leftover debt and lack of responsibility?

12) Why are poverty, ethnicity, & gender likely chosen for special consideration? Are these three any different than choosing people for athletic ability or marching band talent?

13) Is a university by nature an elite institution?—one that caters particularly to "mind power"?

14) Why don't all universities, especially public ones, simply have open enrollments?

15) Is it fair to establish quota systems for classes of people who do especially well on entrance exams and school grades? Why are Asians so successful at competing on a purely intellectual standard?

16) After World War II, the G.I. Bill opened the doors to a college education to millions of veterans, including many who did not have much academic success in high school. Despite many misgivings by some university presidents, the program proved itself an academic success story. What does this experience say about the importance of high school grades? About maturity? About readiness and motivation? And about selection?

17) Baterman's position on enlarging the applicant pool and reserving 50 percent of freshman class spaces to be chosen by lottery raises an important challenge to college administration and admissions. Would his system be "fairer"? Fairer to whom? Would it work? Why might it be resisted?

18) What does Greg mean by saying that a lottery is "equally unfair"?—and thus fair? Could you better accept a rejection based on a lottery than one dictated by present standards of college selection?

19) What does Jaime Sanchez mean by "role models for others to follow"?

20) For whose benefit are the mandates of affirmative action?

21) Civil rights calls for equal protection of the law. Is equality a desirable goal for society? For a public university supported by public tax money? For private colleges and universities which accept public funds? How about equality in terms of availability of service to all the public?

Introduction: Case # 3—The Safety Net

The case-study that follows is composed of reader replies to a newspaper article written by an educated welfare-recipient. The article that prompted the outpouring of letters pro and con is purposely left out so the case readers have the opportunity to piece together what the original article is trying to say to the public. As the discussion of the case evolves, the task broadens to an examination of definitional problems in the sample letters selected for inclusion in the case-study. Finally, the case forces judgments to be made about the facts and value questions posed by the author of the article and the responding letter writers. Note that the names have been changed to protect the privacy of all concerned.

Get yourself a large 3-ring notebook and do so for each course you are going to teach. The format of Case #3 highlights the vital need of teachers to be consummate collectors of problem-posing materials—readings, letters, films, cartoons, records, anecdotes, lab samples, plays etc. that can energize the teaching/learning process and wean teaching away from too great a dependence on expository and formulaic textbooks. The more problem-posing the material, the better. This resource file should grow with each passing year of teaching as a function of changing times and new developments in the field of study. Interesting cases and other materials can and should be contributed by both students and teacher, in a joint endeavor to keep a course alive and current, as well as reflective of the issues from the past that open the door to insights of historical and artistic importance. For convenience, store the best on your computer.

Face the fact that some materials that once worked well may have become dated; that resources, even current ones, have no guarantees. What works well with one class may not work at all with another. The beauty of the 3-ring notebook is that it is open for the new and different, for experimentation, and for easy discard or filing away of materials no longer relevant or useful; or ones which the teacher has grown weary of using. Teaching should be a growth experience and the degree of development can often be measured in the resource file collected and used by any given teacher.

3. The Shrinking Safety Net

A. Poor, poor Angela Judson. I refer to her article on your editorial pages. The meager amount she receives from Aid to Families with Dependent Children is so inadequate that she is reduced to fasting three or four days each week. She says that she is ashamed to take money from the state. But, she says she cannot allow her child to grow thin.

Her AFDC and food stamps benefits are so inadequate that she has been driven to such extreme money-conserving measures as not buying deodorant and not shaving her legs so as not to buy razor blades unnecessarily. This is sad! What are the poor and helpless of this world to do when they must deal with such an unfair welfare system?

All right. Let's take a look at the other side of this story. This woman has been educated at a public university, where she is currently a graduate student. As part of her educational benefits, she admits she received student grants and loans as well as research fellowships. She owns a gas-guzzling car. She admits her rent is not as cheap as it might be. She has a telephone. One must conclude from her article that the reason she is on the dole in the first place is so that she can qualify for public assistance to further her education. The one thing she does not have that would probably meet all of her needs is a job.

Angela Judson is exactly the type of person the welfare reform politicians are rightfully trying to discourage from going onto welfare. If she cares so much for her child, and if she is so concerned about her meager existence, she should leave graduate school, get a job, and stop complaining.   R.H.G.

B. Angela Judson attempts to elicit reader sympathy…Granted, she is my fellow human being, but I am not at all convinced that I, as a taxpayer should pay for her chosen lifestyle. Judson is an articulate, well-educated person. I have no doubt that she could land a good entry-level job making $1,400 a month or more. She doesn't need to put up with meager state offerings.

She can go to night school and get that post-graduate degree if she really wants to further herself. Many others have done it.

But Judson, who admits she "miscalculated time and money" and ended up on welfare, has miscalculated again—she doesn't see the need to get a job.

Maybe Judson has her reasons for not wanting to soil her hands with working in the here and now. Maybe she has valid grounds for wanting to get a master's degree in political science, a field not known for its practicality or wage earning potential. It's not up to me to question the way she chooses to run her life. But then it's not up to her to ask me to foot the bill.   Harold G.

C. Have I been had? Is this a bizarre takeoff by the children of the 1960's to befuddle us children of the 1930's? Sorry, but empathy is impossible; the gulf between us is too wide!...

Whatever became of the idea that you took the work you could get and made the best of it?...I looked at the Sunday classified ads and there were hundreds of jobs available for dozens of (technical) skills...-but there wasn't a single job for a person with a graduate degree in political science! Political scientists are a drug on the market. I can't seem to get it through my head why my tax dollars are supporting people going after political science degrees...when the country needs people with high tech skills to keep us competitive with the rest of the world...

          JNL

D. I wonder how many voters switched after reading this article. Here we have Judson who has accepted, by her own count, student grants and loans, research fellowships, public education to the university post-graduate level, cheap public transportation, and other public (spell that taxpayer) benefits...

She has miscalculated her time and money...I wonder what the marketability is for the poli-sci major. The usual goal is elective office...

She found herself in a violent, sick marriage, with a young child to support. Did her marriage start out violent and sick, or did it get that way somewhere along the way of her university studies? Failed at marriage, trying to mix university studies with child-raising, she expects the working people to put her through post-graduate work. Then, if she reaches her goal, she can appropriate and spend our money, and tell us how to live. These are the only things that politicians do.

So we have a non-supporting father, a post-graduate student and an innocent, hungry, ill-clothed child. Which of these are we supposed to feel compassion and generosity for? The answer is obvious. The solution is also obvious: Get a Legislature and a Supreme Court that will compel parents to support their children. How can Angela Judson expect the taxpayers to support her and her daughter when her own priorities have post-graduate studies ahead of "real work" and supporting her daughter?...?   Ned S.

Sample of replies to the first batch of letters:

E. I am saddened and angered by all the letters to <u>The Times</u>, "Life in the Shrinking Safety Net." Those rugged individualists display an utter lack of compassion or understanding for the plight of Angela Judson, who is a recipient of Aid to Families with Dependent Children.

This is a case of a woman who is obviously talented and ambitious but who is TEMPORARILY forced to accept welfare.... Is higher learning for a professional career only for those who can afford the tuition? Angela Judson should be encouraged for her ambition and determination.

Most people who are on welfare are ashamed of their circumstances and want to get off as soon as possible. I know, because my mother, my sister and I were helped after my father died when I was 12. When I graduated from high school at 18, I managed to find work at the beginning of the Great Depression and held onto it for dear life even though I hated my job. I'm proud to have become the breadwinner of my family at such an early age. I'm very grateful to the welfare system that made it possible for me to at least graduate from high school.

Angela Judson does not deserve the insensitive criticism of the letter writers.... As she says, she expects to find a job soon and pay back in taxes what she received in welfare. She will become a productive citizen and family provider....   L. Grigel

F. The angry respondents to Angela Judson's article must be unaware of a few things that have changed in this country in the last 50 years.

Inexpensive apartments in safe neighborhoods are gone. The chances of obtaining an entry-level job that will cover day-care costs and the basic expenses of raising a child are on par with winning the lottery. If she is to give up her telephone and car, as some readers suggested, her opportunity to find a job is that much less.

However, these suggestions were downright compassionate compared to the one reader who felt Judson should have stayed with her violent husband. Dead mothers and children are no burden to the taxpayer.   Cherie T.

G. I am incensed about the attitude of some Americans toward people on welfare. These people only heard what they wanted to hear from the article and ignored the truth.

They didn't listen when Judson said she couldn't move from her too expensive apartment. She doesn't have the money to pay for moving expenses or the deposit on a new apartment. Where do they want her to get the money? Should she get rid of the phone? I guess people on welfare shouldn't be allowed the safety of having a telephone.

They criticize her for having a gas-guzzling car. People who have money don't realize how hard it is to get $1,800 or $1,900 together to buy a car, and a gas-guzzler is all that one will get for that price. Have these people ever tried to use the bus system to do all of their shopping, errands, laundry, and also to get to work or school? Of course, one reader speaks of his struggle through graduate school with the help of his wife. Could he have made it if it was just him and his three kids? Perhaps, but then we would have to take the male/female wage differential into account.

Angela doesn't have anyone but the people of the United States to help her. These letter writers are a sorry lot. D.T.O.

H. Don't some of your readers have anything better to do than attack a single mother trying to rear a child and make her way through graduate school? In a country that is spending billions to build weapons, support dictators that suppress their people, give charity loans to bail out floundering corporations, etc., this woman hardly seems like a major problem.

Do only the rich and privileged have the right to study and understand political science? Are they the only ones who have the right to prepare themselves to assume a leadership role in our society? If this woman has the intelligence and perseverance to be accepted into and make it halfway through graduate school, it would seem society could give her a helping hand. Being forced to accept a job she's overqualified for or go to school only part time seems hardly an intelligent solution. Rodney M.

(All letters quoted from the *Los Angeles Times*, November 13 and 24, 1984: edited and paraphrased—all names used are fictional).

Vocabulary: social "safety net"; AFDC; food stamps; children of the 60's; marketable skills; poli-sci job opportunities; a "productive" citizen; child support; affirmative action; economic democracy.

Discussion: Which of the following questions should first be thrown on the table by the discussion leader for priority attention:

1) Is Ms. Reading a social misfit?

2) Is she an example of how fate changes the best laid plans of people and government?

3) Why is Ms. Reading asking for public aid?

4) What events in her life greatly affected her plans?

5) Should a person with a B.A. degree be barred from any further public support on the ground that the degree makes one solely responsible for getting on with life and making a living?

6) Should the government make Ms. Reading change to a more practical course with readily marketable skills as a condition of further financial aid? What are the letter writers most upset about with respect to Ms. Readings article and plea?

7) Should people "gut out" bad marriages and tough situations for the sake of the children? Should they learn to take *any* job or should they refuse work outside their interests and training?

8) What are the defenders of Ms. Reading saying in answer to her critics? Do they have a point?

9) Are Ms. Readings defenders simply idealistic "do-gooders"-Or socialists?

Why do they defend her?

10) Should one be ashamed to be on welfare?

11) What kind of jobs would one be qualified for with a degree in political science? Is this a legitimate field of study for a poor person?

12) What daily costs would an unmarried or divorced parent have to bear that would make their life financially difficult?

13) Is public support of Ms. Reading and her child in the long run best public interest?

14) Is she on the road to becoming "a productive citizen?"

4. A Case of "Junk Food"

Complaints by a growing minority of parents and some teachers had led the Board of Education of Plainview School District to appoint a special committee to consider the matter of overly sweet and fatty foods in school vending machines and cafeterias. The Committee on Nutrition and Education, formed in cooperation with the P.T.A., spent six months visiting schools, interviewing parents, students, and teachers, and generally becoming acquainted with nutritional studies, before submitting a report which recommended the phasing out of "junk food" in vending machines over a three year period and a Spring cutback of fifty percent in the amount of fat allowed in meals prepared in school cafeterias. Two of the nine committee members refused to sign the report, saying that the action intended was too drastic, and that the proper way to proceed was through better public education on nutrition.

The matter came to a head one October evening in a large auditorium used for public hearings on topics of wide public interest. A formal proposal in line with the recommendations of the Committee on Nutrition and Education was introduced by Committeewoman Alexis Darron. Ms. Darron proceeded to summarize the main facts and findings: The percentage of overweight people in the U.S. population is growing and that means more health problems, higher costs to society, and a good deal of unhappiness. Research evidence shows dramatically that overweight teenagers grow into overweight adults, and that the time to make people aware of the importance of good nutrition and staying fit is especially during the school years. Yet, the Committee discovered that school lunches routinely were very high in fats, desserts were particularly sugary, and as much as eighty percent of the food in vending machines is rightfully classed as "junk food."

Further, because of the influence of television and cars, young people were not exercising as much as their parents did. Also, many food businesses were taking advantage of the young people by cleverly advertising soft drinks and meals that plainly did not meet the standards of good nutrition. Spot commercials and glossy magazines freely distributed to the kiddie and teen-age market were aimed at creating and sustaining eating fads, a fact underscored by the "get with it" themes and by the booming sales of "playfood"—usually plastic replicas of actual fast foods and junk foods for youngsters to play with. Figuring an allowance of perhaps three dollars a week for millions of American kids (far more than that in Plainview) means a market of almost five BILLION dollars a year. That is an irresistible target for the advertisers, and unfortunately junk food ads dominate the food messages sent to school children. There is simply no way the educational system can advance nutritional truth and a balance of views, Ms. Darron concluded, short of drastic action that cuts off the supply of unhealthy foods and that models correct nutritional choices.

At this point, the floor was opened to questions and short comments by anyone present. For ninety minutes, school board members sat at rapt attention listening to a variety of views both favoring and opposing the proposal. The opposition was perhaps best summarized by a Mr. Stan Garvey, who had several children attending the Plainview schools and who was a well known and respected businessman. Food choices, said Mr. Garvey, "are not a matter for a school board to legislate, but are clearly the province of each parent." A school board can and should urge the teaching of good nutrition, but should not go so far as to limit the choice of students and parents; that in effect would amount to a boycott of certain products. In a free society the individual must learn to choose for himself and the greater good is obtained by maintaining a free market. When enough people become dissatisfied with the food choices available, they will stop buying the offending products and the manufacturers and suppliers will respond to the change in demand.

Furthermore, Mr. Garvey contended, the Plainview schools had a fine athletic and health program which is perfectly capable of teaching good nutrition. Obviously the winning teams of Plainview and the exuberance of its young people are testimony to the success of school health programs. Indeed, the vast majority of teachers could be seen eating in the school cafeteria and buying the very same foods as the children purchased from the vending machines. Perhaps those machines could be stocked somewhat more with fresh fruits and yogurts, but the evidence indicated that these items would not be among the major purchases.

Income from campus vending machines and from the student store contributes heavily to support of school sports and extra-curricular activities, Mr. Garvey noted, and no one at this meeting would want to see those programs harmed by a drop in receipts. Restrictions on food supplies on campus would not work in any case, because students would still buy what pleases them in off-campus stores or bring it from home. And beyond certain general cautions, who can guarantee what is healthy eating and what is not, Mr. Garvey asked the audience. "We all know people who lived to eighty or ninety and who ate everything and anything, while others who took great care about their diet died at a much earlier age. So by all means, let's continue with Plainfield's fine health program, and even beef up the curriculum in nutrition. But let's leave the decision on what to eat to the parents and students. It is the consumer, not the school district, who ultimately and rightfully has to make the choice in a free society."

School board President Eldon, who had not actively supported the work of the Committee on Nutrition and Education, asked Ms. Darron to make a very brief rebuttal considering the lateness of the hour. In her three minute statement she again pointed to the power of advertising over the consumer and denied that a free market could exist in the schools given that kind of influence. But even if it could, she asked the audience, "Do not the schools stand for something better?—as models for the best in health education and training, for keeping up with the latest scientific findings."

In places as different as Singapore (Trim and Fit Program), Finland (campaign to reduce heart disease) and Berkeley, California (education for healthy eating) major positive health changes have resulted from education. Early-established nutritional habits last a lifetime, just as there is a direct relationship between poor nutritional habits and poor health. Rising health care costs result. Quality of life is severely damaged by bad or indifferent nutrition education.

Those who are resistant to change should be faced with these real problems and the fact that there are intelligent options for solving them. Students, teachers, parents, and board members should not be burying their heads in the sand about the health care crisis and long run costs. Also, school money should not dictate health policy, she concluded. For we can make even more money for sports and extra-curriculars by selling drugs and related items in campus stores and vending machines. That we do not do so is not because those items can also be purchased off-campus, but because we stand as a school for something better. "Are we so hypocritical as to teach the theory of good health, but not its practice?"

With all sides having been heard, the school board adjourned to private quarters for a half-hour of closed deliberations before reassembling for a final hour of public debate and a vote. What should they decide to do?

Discussion:

1) How would you define "junk food"? How does society pay the greater cost of overweight?

2) If the problem is as serious as described, why are not more teachers and parents actively engaged in changing the curriculum and food service?

3) Is the task of the schools mainly that of giving information and expanding knowledge—or role modeling and changing behavior?

4) To what extent has advertising upset the balance of information necessary to a free marketplace of ideas?

5) If not through drastic actions such as those advocated by the Committee on Nutrition and Education, how else might the school system teach students to become more nutritionally selective?

6) Is this case mainly a result of long years of parent neglect, teacher neglect, or the lack—until recently—of sound scientific evidence?

7) How would you respond to the contention that "we all know people of 80 or 90 who ate everything and anything…"?

8) Since students can and do bring from home what they cannot buy in school, should the education effort be more directed to the parents than the students?

9) Should parents have a right to make meal choices for themselves and their children even if that runs counter to good nutrition and scientific findings?

10) Is income from campus vending machines and the student store a legitimate consideration for school authorities? How should this be balanced against the need for healthy food service?

11) Supposing that one or two new vending machines offering only nutritionally sound foods were added to those already on campus. Would that likely solve the problem?

12) Do bad food choices, like bad money, drive out the good?

13) Are the successes of Plainview's sports program a convincing argument against major reform?

14) At what point should schools enter into the realms of social action?—Or should they? At what point is failure to act an admission of hypocrisy?

15) What did Mr. Garvey mean by saying that in a free society, people must learn to choose for themselves? Given the preponderance of advertising for nutritionally inferior foods, have we already given up our freedom of choice?

16) What should the school board do?

5. A Case of Culture Shock and Immigration Policy

In the Tri-cities area, as in many of our urban centers, waves of immigration from abroad overburdened the schools and led to drastic changes in scheduling and student assignment. Some schools moved to year-round schedules as a way of trying to cope with the problems of overcrowding and double sessions. Others, such as Pembroke High became part of a massive bussing program aimed at reducing the load on inner city areas by distributing students to the less populated schools on the urban fringe.

A byproduct of the bussing program and the immigration surge was the shift of neighborhood children to private schools. At Pembroke and its two feeder junior highs, the flight of area-resident children was increasing with each year. At present, fully fifty percent of the freshman class is composed of youngsters transported from distant locations. In many respects, it is a replay of the late 1970's, when court ordered mandatory bussing to achieve racial integration also led to suburban white flight. The revival of the public suburban neighborhood schools was stimulated by the termination of the mandatory bussing order in 1980, the substitution of a voluntary program, and the introduction of five magnet schools. The latter tended to achieve a fair measure of integration by attracting a racial and ethnic mix of students to those schools with particular curriculum specialties such as the fine arts or science. And many inner-city parents and children chose, in any case, to bus out to the suburbs as a way of avoiding crowded central city schools with their attendant problems.

Now, with the growing population surge, all the Tri-city schools once again have come under tremendous pressure. With open enrollment, fifteen thousand students per day are already bussed to suburban schools, almost half of these traveling eighteen miles or more each way. Many of these youngsters are struggling to learn English, and to become acculturated to their new country. And the situation at Pembroke High is typical, with but two teachers fairly fluent in a language other than English (only Spanish and French), while many of the newcomers speak such languages as Farsi, Chinese, Portuguese, Hebrew, Korean, Armenian, and Vietnamese. The need for translators and special books and supplies and the constant checking in of new students led to disruptions in schedules and routines and an atmosphere of concern on the part of neighborhood parents. The middle class and affluent community is deeply worried about maintaining standards for college entrance and about the noise and confusion that have become part of the daily routine.

So it was that on a Tuesday in April, a small group of Pembroke neighborhood PTA parents, students, and teachers were invited to a meeting at the Tricities school board. Also present were two English-speaking parents of immigrant children attending Pembroke schools. Superintendent Boyd McAlister began with a short summary of the enrollment situation, while noting that everyone present had an interest in maintaining Pembroke as a high quality school. He asked Elizabeth Gladden, a Pembroke High alumnus and now a member of the P.T.A., to offer her view of the situation as a focus for discussion:

"It is very easy to speak of the need for ethnic balance in the schools and of serving the needs of immigrant children. I agree. But when it comes to the practicality of doing this, I have certain difficulty…and I am not alone given the outflow of neighborhood children. A school runs smoothly when it represents a community. Everyone concerned works together and we all get to know each other both off and on the school grounds. Such is no longer the case at Pembroke, which sometimes feels like a bus station in a strange land. It's interesting, but is it effective educationally? So far, I've kept my children at Pembroke schools and I'd like to see them graduate from Pembroke High. But I'm frankly worried about the decline in standards. My kids are getting superior grades, but the quality of their education is less than what I got. Perhaps every parent feels this way and glamorizes their own school experience. But both my son and daughter tell me that their classes are continually slowed down by the need to constantly re-explain the simplest concepts. Further, there is a lot of confusion and fooling around, which the teachers seem helpless to deal with. The academic enrichment courses run much more smoothly, but even here standards have slipped. With all the attention to language and cultural problems, which are important, the overall atmosphere of the school is not academic. I don't know how else to put it. The Pembroke community is simply losing interest in the school. And for a school with a long tradition, it's a shame to see it going this way."

"I agree that there is a problem," put in Spanish and home economics teacher Claire Calaro, "but it is not as bad as what appears. After all, this country has been through all this before with the immigrants of our parent's generation. What we need is more bi-lingual teachers and more emphasis on bi-cultural education. The students are getting a marvelous cross-cultural experience that does count for a lot in life, even though it is not on a high school transcript for college. We have to change the way we measure an education. Anyway, I think the whole thing will settle down in a year or two, if people would just not panic."

"That's easy for you to say," interjected science teacher Lori Pauling. Language and culture is your specialty Claire, but even you can't speak to all these language groups. In other areas of curriculum, it is very hard to get discussion moving and to keep student attention focused. Some immigrant groups do fantastic, work even harder than our regular Pembroke kids. But many from the central city are not motivated to learn, whether immigrant or native born. It is the college-bound who end up being cheated, and they are leaving us for the private schools. We do try to reach all the kids, but it is an impossible task given our resources. I do understand the concerns of the local kids."

"Their parent's concerns, more likely!" Kevin Atherton, a senior, broke in. "I see it both ways. I've learned a bit about people different than myself, and through them I've learned more about the world. You can't just get that from a textbook, you know. On the other hand, my friends are all achievers, regardless of background. The problem is really one of social class. A lot of the inner city kids don't have the family supports and push; they don't have the motivation for long-term rewards or the close knit family that propels them to achieve academically. The college-bound mix more easily with us Pembroke people. The rest segregate themselves by language, race, or nationality, and you can see them, especially on the lunch-court, jabbering away at selected tables. They sit together for security, I suppose, but it defeats the goal of learning English and mixing. Well, I suppose I should try more to extend my friendship circle, but I have just so much time. I try to meet and befriend people who are on my wavelength."

Mrs. Lee, one of the invited immigrant parents, was given a nod of recognition by Superintendent McAlister. "I appreciate your honesty, Kevin. And I am happy you made friends with my son, and helped him feel at home at Pembroke. My family is fortunate. We are well off and have a long tradition of education. We have to remember how many children are not so lucky, how many are confused and upset by the huge changes and the hurdle of learning new traditions and a new language. For their parents it is often even worse. We have to imagine how hard it must be for a family struggling along with little, and seeing their children being absorbed into a culture they only dimly understand and may not accept. It is not easy. We must somehow help the local neighborhood people of Pembroke better understand the problem and give them encouragement to stick by us newcomers."

"If we had a magic wand, we could do that," Miss Pauling responded. But we are all under the gun of college entrance. It's the colleges and universities that create the intense pressure on the high schools and that cause the parents to react with alarm. Anyway it is not mainly immigrant kids that I see as the problem. So many of them are among our best students. The problem is what has happened to our general American values. Education is just not respected. Only grades seem to count. Diplomas and degrees are just another status symbol, not a mark of interest and excellence. Get rich quick! Have it all now! The "me" generation....

"I agree that it is a much deeper issue than it seems at first glance," Mrs. Gladden put in. Indeed, it is federal immigration policy, or the lack of it, that has thrown this problem on the local schools. But while all these issues are very important, they are tangential to our main concern today. The question is how do we maintain standards at Pembroke and how do we stem neighborhood flight?"

"You stem it," shot back another of the Pembroke teachers, "by insuring the parents around the Pembroke school that they are not going to send their kids to a school dominated by various minorities. That is the root of their concern and I don't see how you are going to change it unless we agree to import only English-speaking Einstein's to Pembroke High."

That comment erupted into twenty minutes of heated discussion over academic standards, who is really interested in education, what is the nature of "real education," and the issue of crumbling neighborhood support. The school Superintendent rapped on the table and smiled. "Well" we really have the juices flowing—and I love it! We have created a fine course now in all the Great Issues in Education. And that's good, because we are making progress in a democratic way.

"We need now to focus, and I feel we have the germ of a few practical ideas for change. For example, I note Kevin's passing thought about lunch table self-segregation. Well, could we agree to have one day a week for special lunch table assignments at which we make sure to get a mix of students? Or how about senior honor students being required to serve as tutorial leaders in some of the harder subjects and in English? We can make sure that all freshmen and sophomores attend these study circles as part of their course credit. Can we get twenty—or forty—bi-lingual parents to serve as teacher-aides? I'm sure there is a lot of untapped talent out there in the community.

"How can the university help us, and can we help them? And what can we do at Pembroke to get central city parents and neighborhood parents to meet on some regular schedule and work together?"

"I'd like to get your thoughts on some specific action plans, because I want to put them into effect as soon as possible. I want to hear some good ideas on ways to turn things around. What do you have to recommend?"...

Discussion:

1) What is meant by a "neighborhood school"? Does the term mean only the area within, say, a mile of a school or can it be used to imply a whole section or suburb of a city? Can it mean the entire city?

2) Is a diversity of language groups a divisive or a unifying factor in education? Is language diversity well utilized in American education? What of cultural diversity?—is that a plus factor in American education?

3) Is the withdrawal of neighborhood students from the Pembroke schools motivated more by unrealistic fears or by a realistic appraisal of educational opportunities?

4) Are the universities contributing to or causing the disruption in secondary education by holding to overly high grade standards in a time of great social change? Could the universities adopt a better admissions standard than high school grades and-test scores?

5) Since it is federal immigration policy that has led to the surge in immigration and attendant overcrowding of urban schools, should the federal government be required to pay for all the resulting increased costs and mitigation efforts?

6) Mrs. Gladden admits that people tend to glamorize their own school experiences. What psychological factors operate on the older generation to make them want their children to duplicate their own real or imagined experiences?

7) The teacher, Ms. Calaro, thinks that we have to change the way we measure an education. What exactly does she imply?

8) Is social segregation, such as is seen at lunch tables, a natural form of grouping or is it imposed by feelings of acceptance and rejection? Would once-a-week table assignments work to break down the isolation?

9) Year round schools will reduce the need for bussing, but will it increase the degree of segregation at Tri-cities schools? Is segregation by language or class status any less unfair to students than segregation by race or sex? Does segregation by language or social class create a feeling of inferiority in the students? Does it lead to feelings of superiority in the higher achieving suburban schools?

10) Mrs. Lee spoke up for the many displaced people and their children who have a host of problems and great struggle to integrate into American life. Is the school the proper agency to deal with these problems? If not, what institutions should take command? And what part should the schools play in easing problems of acculturation?

11) Should outreach to the larger community be a main focus of secondary education? Is the function of curriculum to teach mainly the history and theories of social change or to become part of the process?

12) Is Superintendent McAlister facing the problem of community support realistically? Is he casting stones at the sea?

13) Would the Pembroke High community be more supportive of the high school if "English-speaking Einsteins" constituted the main flow of the bussed-in students? Or would that too be seen as a threat to the college entrance possibilities of local youngsters?

14) Will more bi-lingual aids solve the problems of Pembroke High?

15) Is Superintendent McAlister the kind of leader you would like to work with?

16) What kind of suggestions for dealing with the problems of Pembroke are likely to be thrown on the table? And what are your own suggestions for specific action?

10

Testing and Grading

Preparing and administering examinations and evaluating student performance are key elements of the teacher role. The testing process can be a powerful tool for learning and a spirited way of advancing motivation and analysis. Poorly prepared, the testing process is but a tiresome and distasteful chore for teachers and students, with negative effects on interest in subject matter.

A principal aim of educating is greater and sharpened critical thinking. It is therefore counter-productive, even nonsensical, to offer tests and other evaluation instruments that do not encourage analysis and creative effort. Examinations that reinforce mainly fact-regurgitation are one of the worst offenders on the road to dulling the school experience. Good testing often includes fact-recognition and recall, but by and large it reaches for meanings, causes, and implications.

True-false testing reduces life and thought to simple alternatives that encourage guessing and penalize the good thinkers, who see varied angles and probe more deeply into issues than those presented as black or white choices. Multiple-choice questions (more accurately called by students, "multiple-guess") make the grading process much easier, but also foster random choosing of answers and surface skimming that discourages original thinking and analysis; the answer choices are presented to the learner and thereby creativity is pushed aside. This also encourages teaching to the test (the "right" answers) and leaves the false appearance of intellectual performance. The results are a smokescreen hiding a grossly inferior education. At intermediate and earlier grade levels, it can be considered a modern form of child-abuse.

In real life, when your car suddenly stops running as a function of some problem, a card does not appear on the windshield asking: a. it's the radiator; b. it's the alternator; c. it's the sparkplugs; d. it's the tires; e. it's none of the above…. Real life demands that the driver assess the gauges, eliminate alternatives that do not bear on engine performance, and postulate possibilities for restarting the engine. Most of life's problems demand some original investigation (perhaps leafing through the "Troubleshooting" chapter in the Driver's Manual). Soon one comes up with some sense of the problem and begins to try different things. Of course, unlike the rules of the examination room, the easy choice is to immediately surrender thinking and phone the Auto Club and its experts, who do constitute a good last resort.

I am amazed and sometimes discouraged at how easily educators give in to what has become standardized "objective testing," and do not even consider the advantages and creativity to be found in many alternative forms of questions that can make the evaluation process insightful and even enjoyable for the students. Creative teaching demands creative questioning and a reinforcement of inductive thinking by both students and teachers.

What follows are some examples of a variety of questioning techniques that can be used to change the traditional emphasis on simple fact and recognition to higher processes of thinking that ask for meanings, implications, causes, possibilities. Some of these test questions simply elevate the dialogue by creating situations in which the learner has to go a step or two further than simple recognition or recall, and has to state the reasons and make the connections. The goal here and now is to offer examples and pathways which you, the instructor, can add to or take-off from in devising your own problem-centered curriculum.

We'll begin with a very simple example of changing a question of recall to one that reinforces learning and probes for deeper meaning. You can be sure that the following question or some variation of it has appeared on hundreds of American history tests:

<u>What were the names of the three ships that sailed with Columbus</u>?

The problem is that the names of three ships are really not that important historically, and, worse, recall of the correct names does not in any way insure a grasp of destinations, motives, expansionary policies etc, which are quite important. In this instance, I prefer to state the fact as part of the question asked and then ask the learner for some aspect of interpretation. For example:

"We all know that Columbus sailed with three ships, the Nina, the Pinta, and the Santa Maria. But what was his destination and what did he hope to find there?" Or: "What surprising news about his discovery would Columbus bring back to Spain?

Similarly, the question, "What invention made Eli Whitney famous?" can be upgraded to produce critical thinking: "Eli Whitney is famous for his invention of the cotton gin. Why might historians feel it a tragedy that his invention did not come thirty years earlier?"—as one example.

Almost every exam will have some factual recall elements. But these should not dominate the questioning process, especially as the teacher is trying to reinforce a pattern of reflective and analytical thinking. Now, let us move on to review a variety of approaches to questioning that aims at helping the learner to ponder reasons, meanings, interpretations, and logical sense:

A) From a conservation standpoint, certain actions are either economical or Diseconomical (sound or unsound). Explain which and why in three lines or less for each item:

1) An Eskimo makes an aluminum blade knife from the wreckage of an airplane.

2) A housewife drives her husband's truck two blocks to mail a letter.

3) A landscaper plants tall evergreen trees on the south side of a new apartment house.

Note: Reasonable line limits are imposed to insure answers are pointed and illustrative, and so avoid beating around the bush.

B) Supposing you were put in charge of designing a completely new city. How would your new city plan avoid repeating the single greatest energy-wasting mistake of so many of today's cities?
Supposing the U.S. could send nuclear waste in rockets to the sun or bury it in deep salt caverns in desert areas. Explain the nature of risk associated with each approach.
Supposing a petitioner was giving out leaflets on a public street, but many of the recipients respond by crumbling them and dropping the papers on the sidewalk. A policeman warns the pamphleteer about the growing trash. Later, he cites her for continuing to cause litter in and around the area. What Constitutional argument can the petitioner (or her attorney) best present to the court to defend her actions?

C) You are hearing certain loud conversations at a nearby table in a restaurant. In each case, decide if the person speaking is "well informed" or "poorly informed"—and briefly explain why:

1) "Federal aid to American education began with the G.I. Bill after World War II."

2) "Although the women's liberation movement has had many good effects, it has also helped drain public education of a traditional source of highly talented teachers."

3) "In the U.S. most electricity is a product of hydropower and nuclear generation."

D) Complete the following sentences in no more than two lines each. Be sure to offer a clear explanation.

1) Comparison of European and American high school student performance on achievement tests is generally unfair because:

2) Under federal law a "wilderness" is distinct from a "national park" by virtue of:

3) In the Kansas v. Garber (Amish) case, the state claimed it was reinforcing the real purpose of education. Thus, the state argued that it was aiding all students to:

E) Rewrite each of the following objectives that are not set forth as performance goals. If a given objective is stated in performance terms, simply mark "pass" on the appropriate line of your answer sheet:

1) Students will appreciate the physical benefits of brisk walking.

2) Students will find the height of a building by utilizing the shadow on the-ground of a six foot long garden stake.

3) Students will know how important it is to vote in a democratic election.

F) Explain the <u>differences</u> in outcome or meaning in each of the following comparisons. Limit your answers to five lines or less:

1) The difference between the segregation ruling in Plessy v. Ferguson and the 1954 Brown v. Board of Education cases is enormous. How was the 1954 ruling by comparison so different—and what made the newer ruling so difficult to evade?

2) The difference between preaching and teaching can be viewed in terms of educational goals: Preachers have found the truth and feel they must convince the people. In contrast, what is the goal of great teachers?

3) Comparing the advantages of television versus books, it is evident that the former quickly focuses and holds attention and presents scenes that quickly pass time and generation barriers. Nonetheless, what advantages do books offer in stimulating creativity in ways not easily provided by television? (By setting reasonable line limits for student answers, the teacher insures an even playing field. Some students will insist on rambling on, and the way to deal with this is not to impose penalties or get into fruitless argument. Simply state that the limit allows reasonable space for a good and pointed answer and that in order to be fair to all the test-takers only the first five lines of answer will be read and assessed. Or four lines or…)

G) In answering the following questions, offer specific examples:

a) Name two American journals or magazines focused on hard science, and two on popular science. What's the difference?

b) The minimally educated often lead diminished lives because of lack of formal training. Yet, the college educated cannot afford to crow about their wisdom. Give two examples of enormous failures in decision-making by the college educated that negatively affected American society.

c) Two different types of films are showing at local theatres. One is a satire poking fun at politicians; the other is a cop picture featuring blondes, guns, and car chases. How would the philosopher, Mortimer Adler, view adult attendance at these films in terms of 1) recreation; and 2) leisure.

H) Complete the following sentences in two lines, giving a sharp explanation:

1) Middle-class flight to private schools is worrisome to educators who appreciate the historic role of public schools, namely—

2) In many ways, classroom control is a function of hidden messages sent inadvertently by the teacher to the students. For example, teachers who don't do lesson planning will often convey to students—

3) In finding school segregation unconstitutional, the Supreme Court fixed on both a legal and a psychological reason. The psychological reason is—

Having now proceeded through eight examples of upgrading questions to avoid emphasizing mainly recognition and factual recall, and focusing instead on problem-orientation and sharpening judgment, it is well to summarize by examining a last example of question limitations and potential. I choose the well-known area of American government and the limitations of approaching it structurally rather than via problems. Time and again, students of civics and social studies and political science have been drilled with the principle of three great branches of American government, the legislative, the executive, and the judicial. While we can hope that most adults can mouth the names of the three divisions, I have found by testing that less than one in twenty has even the vaguest idea of what it all means in practicality. True, a relatively few people questioned can respond with the drilled statement that the legislative makes the laws, the judicial interprets, and the executive serves to enforce the laws. But what in reality does it all mean?—Is it but a recitation of platitudes, or to be kind, a maxim? We test this with problem-orientation, as in the following (and I'm willing to bet that most people have never before thought of the branches of government in these practical terms):

> The principle of three coordinating but independent branches of government is rooted in American Constitutional law. For each of the following examples, distinguish whether the action described is carried out within (1) the executive; (2) the legislative; or (3) the judicial branch. Also (to avoid the multiple-guess syndrome) explain in no more than two lines, why the branch of government chosen is responsible for that particular action:
>
> a) The Patent Office approves the uniqueness of a claimed invention.
>
> b) A man is fingerprinted at FBI headquarters.
>
> c) The Rivers and Harbors Act is amended to include an environmental limit.
>
> d) A request for an injunction is denied.
>
> e) The U.S. Social Security office denies a petition by a 70 year old couple for an increase in benefit payments.

What I am illustrating here is the importance of helping learners see beyond the obvious and reach way past the flip answer. Tests that involve mainly or wholly recall and recognition simply reinforce surface coverage and the patina of learning. Test scores that are made by fast electronic scanning and without review of the meaning of the questions and the answers only encourage teacher laziness and student indifference. They dull the potential for learning how to think and how to judge. And it is no wonder that the forgetting rate is so great, that important information and ways of processing simply are not taught or fade away. When the test scores become more important than the process of approaching issues and problems, both teachers and learners become dulled. Fixated on status, the educational journey loses its validity, as memorization for exams becomes a local mania and a national hysteria. Worse, pushed by bureaucrats, pettifoggers, and powerful test lobbies, many creative teachers opt out of teaching rather than be stifled in forced play of the inane game of test-results bragging.

For the politicians, testing has become a mantra, a sacred cow formula for touting commitment to school reform and educational advancement. It makes for great theatre, but the mania for testing has little value. The vast majority of tests (mainly multiple choice and fact recognition) are nearly worthless in terms of reinforcing critical thinking. They emphasize surface skimming of content, regurgitation and guesswork, and force both students and teachers to partake in a charade of teaching-to-the-tests in order to save face and "prove" they are doing a good job. On both educational and ethical planes, it teaches a wrong lesson. And it is an incredible waste of time and money! Good testing arises from the class-room and not from bureaucrats and education hucksters; indeed, the more they measure, the less they know.

Thus, it is extremely important that exams are reviewed with the class, that questioning and testing are an integral part of the learning process, and not an imposition from afar or from above, an added burden on teachers. Part of the fun of learning is the colloquy that can be carefully nurtured over the logic or illogic of answers and over the very wording of questions. It keeps all parties to the pro-cess on their toes, even as it reinforces learning and sharpens judgment. And it openly admits that we are all capable of error and, hopefully, attuned to learning from mistakes. Better that than the illusion that we have "learned" because of a score, when in fact the learning may be minimal or inconsequential and the criti-cal thinking almost nonexistent. Let us promise to ask intelligent questions on tests as well as in classroom discussion.

Grading

All grading is more or less subjective. No matter how carefully tests are pre-pared and scored, subjectivity is bound to enter the process. The decision of what to accept as a correct answer (or what to score partially correct answers) are sub-jective decisions by the teacher or grader. The ambiguity of some questions and the restrictive effect of offering only certain alternative choices as "correct" adds to the stew. Thus, so-called "objective" tests, rule out differing interpretations of items and overlook important reasoning and argument behind a choice that can be of greater importance than the "correct answer" itself.

But beyond the issue of framing questions and deciding on what constitutes a correct answer is the question of the meaning or measure of the scores. The total score value of points given for correct answers (or points taken off for incorrect responses) is itself a subjective call. And teachers tend not to want to think about this.

Are all the questions to be weighed or scored equally, or are some questions to be given more emphasis or points? Shall partial credit be given for partially-right answers? And, most important, how shall letter grades be assigned on the basis of the scores? It is to this last point that I draw special attention, for final grades do not automatically come out of the clear blue sky. For illustrative purposes, let's look at the following example of a hypothetical test taken by a class (or combined class) of fifty-two students.

Individual scores are noted by "x" or "error points" (the number of points taken off for incorrect answers). In the score sheet shown below the top scorer lost only 3 points, while the lowest scorer lost 57 points. The total possible errors on this test was 112, which would occur if any student was wrong on every question. Now, how would you give letter grades to these 52 students? In other words, where would you draw the line between "A" and "B", between "B" and "C" etc.? We could go still further and ask whether you would allow for pluses and minuses (as in C+ or A-)? But for the sake of simplicity just draw the line right now between the major grades: "A" through "F":

```
                                        X
                X               X       X  X                    X
            X   X   X   X X X       X X X   X     X X X
errors: 0 1 2 3 4 5 6 7 8 9 10 11 12 13 14 15 16 17 18 19 20 21 22 23


X                                       X
X       X   X       X X              X       X     X       X X
X       X     X X     X X       X X X     X X     X X     X X    .
24 25 26 27 28 29 30 31 32 33 34 35 36 37 38 39 40 41 42 43 44 45 46


        X   X
    .   X   X       X           X                                    .
    47 48 49 50 51 52 53 54 55 56 57 58 59 60 ---------------------------112
```

Now, let's look at some examples of letter scoring by teachers with different standards or philosophies of grading:

a) Teacher A feels that only students who score on a test no more than 10 percent wrong (or 90 percent or-higher right answers) should be given a grade of "A". Up to 20 percent wrong (or 80-90 percent right answers) should get a grade of "B". Using this fixed rule the next 10 percent would be marked a "C", the next 10 percent with a "D", and those scoring below 40 percent wrong (or sixty percent correct answers) would fail the test and be given a grade of "F". Under this system there would be no adjustment for the difficulty of the test, nor would grades be "curved" or bent according to any average of student performance. Using this measure, Teacher A would draw the line between letter grades "A" and "B" in the above example at 11 error points (10 percent of the 112 possible errors that could be made on this test). Similarly, he would draw a line at 22 error points for the "B's", 33 points for the "C's" and so forth. His class of 52 students would end up with a total of 5 "A's", 13 "B's", 13 "C's", 13 "D's", and 8 "Fails."

b) Teacher B looks at the scatter of grades, and for a combination of reasons (harder than usual test, accepts some leeway needed in scoring, inadequate time for preparation by students etc.) decides to be somewhat flexible in scoring the break-points between letter grades. He draws the line at 14 between "A's" and "B's", at 27 for the lowest possible "B", at 37 for lowest "C" and at 46 error points for the lowest grade of "D". His class of 52 students ends up with 9 "A's", 19 "B's", 12 "C's", 10 "D's" and 6 "Fails". Note how he obviously looks for breaks between grades in places where no student has scored that particular number of error points.

Other teachers will have still different standards (stiffer or more elastic) than the above two. The point is that while grades can be stated or justified in points, the outcome depends on any given teacher philosophy of grading. And many teachers do not even stop to think about themselves as grade-makers as well as grade givers. The final grade that a student earns depends on a combination of the answers given, the ambiguity or clarity of the questions, the fairness of the questions asked, the grading of the answers, and the grade point philosophy of the teacher. There is simply no evading this conclusion.

What then can a teacher do to maintain fairness in grading and motivate students to keep trying and learning? First, the grading standards of every teacher should be clearly explained to the class. In addition, I urge a supplementary scale where students can earn extra points for intelligent outside of class work and for participation in special panels and reports in class. Here, I would insist there be no copy work or make-work, but only things which add to the class by way of sanctioned auxiliary activities that promote critical thinking, be they book reports, attendance and analysis of events at relevant public forums, laboratory experiments, interviewing, artistic approaches etc. What the balance point should be between exams and supplementary efforts should be well-defined for the class. And finally, to maintain an open atmosphere in the classroom and a strong feeling of a level playing field, answers to exam questions should be carefully reviewed in class. The posting of scores without an accompanying explanation and review is an all too common practice that is anti-educational and abhorrent. It is unfair to the students and a total "cop-out" for the teacher.

Examination questions should offer a full range of difficulty so that slower students are given a fair chance to succeed and even top students remain challenged and alert. Testing should be an interesting learning experience that aids and motivates the students to develop increasing interest in the subject field. If this does not occur, those students would be better off not having taken the course, for lifelong learning is the overall goal of any valid curriculum. Teachers should reflect much more than they do on this long range implication.

Frankly speaking, students will show initial resistance to the kind of questions and testing advocated here. "Where are the true-false and multiple-choice questions we are used to?" they will lament. The teacher's answer: Well, my job is really one of helping you to think critically and sharpen judgment. Those so-called "objective" tests do not lead in that direction. So bear with me, and soon you will learn to trust your own mind to work through problems and to gain confidence in your own abilities. It makes no sense to teach you with critical thinking approaches in our daily classroom work, and then follow this by testing and grading you in a manner that is simple-minded and unfair to your intelligence."

In a matter of weeks, with practice tests and examples in class, the students will accommodate and even revel in their accomplishments. In my experience, I have found that they will realize how much they have been cheated by a system that is designed more for machine scoring than for true learning. And they will develop an independence of thinking and a trust in their own judgments and abilities. Indeed, given even the many advantages of computer-based learning, the accompanying testing and questioning is mainly or wholly of the "objective" variety, almost inherently so, whereas educators who know and support online education nonetheless conclude that the "essence of learning is best done with real people interacting with real ideas." (Gregory Farrington, President of Lehigh University)

How Teachers Perform: A Self-Test

How well do you comprehend the modern teaching concepts set forth in this book? (Answers will be found on pp. 125-126—although I would much prefer that you not look at them for a week, while pondering your own evaluation). LIMIT YOUR ANSWERS TO FIVE LINES PER QUESTION.

1. Supposing that you are a supervisor of student teachers. On a visit to teacher Q, you discover that the lesson plans are little more than notes of the subject matter topics to be covered for the day. As a student of modern teaching, what would you explain to teacher Q about the purpose of a lesson plan?

2. An article expressing a strong opinion has been distributed to the class and ample time has been given for the students to read it. In opening the discussion, what obligation does the teacher/discussion leader have to the author?

3. Ever since the U.S. Surgeon-General officially announced that smoking presents a hazard to human health, much information has been streamed to the public by various media. The relation of smoking to lung cancer and other diseases is today well known, yet people, especially young people, continue to smoke. What educational lesson about teaching (that teachers often ignore) can be learned from the anti-smoking campaign?

4. Teacher R introduces a unit on the Renaissance with pictures of paintings by Michelangelo. She makes a poster-board display, along with three contrasting paintings by medieval artists. She then points out important differences between Medieval and Renaissance art. Students ask a number of good questions, which she carefully answers using the pictures to illustrate. The class discusses the two styles and things they like and dislike. They write a paragraph noting the differences and the reasons for them. What suggestion can be made to teacher R to help make her basic lesson strategy much more effective?

5. Teacher S is having great difficulty getting much of his class to participate in discussion. He asks provocative questions, has good eye contact, and knows when to pause and wait. What is his best move now in class organization to break the silence and open the class into full discussion?

6. Teacher T has a bimetallic strip (a thin piece of metal which is formed by welding two different metals together, perhaps a strip of tin to a strip of cop-

per). To the untrained eye, the bimetallic strip appears as one piece of metal. The two metals expand differently when heated, and thus the strip always bends to the same side, slowly coming back to original shape as it cools. Of course, the teacher knows this, but the students do not. Teacher T begins class with a five minute explanation of the expansion properties of metals and the principle of the bimetallic strip. He has a diagram on the board and he stimulates and answers student questions. He then lights a candle and has several students demonstrate the principle by heating the strip. He reinforces learning with a follow-up discussion. The students wrap up the lesson by writing-up the experiment. You have been asked to evaluate the lesson. What is your most important criticism of the strategy employed by the teacher?

7.   Teacher U has her students read an exchange of letters as a central part of her lesson. Her main objective is stated as follows: "After reading Mr. Green's letter of early resignation and the short note of the Peace Corps country director urging him to stay and continue his valuable work, the students will be able to list three reasons that Mr. Green offered for quitting." Rewrite (change) this objective so that it focuses on the value issue involved, rather than on the fact level, where it now is.

8.   The verbal activities of the traditional classroom teacher have often been described as consisting largely of TELLING and EXPLAINING. By contrast, what two words might well be used to characterize the problem-centered or modern teacher?

9.   Why do so many teachers, accustomed to the habits of polite conversation, have difficulty adjusting to eye-contact in discussion-leading?

10. Teacher V has his students develop their own montage about how something works. It can be mechanical, biological, or psychological. The cutout pictures and drawings are mounted on poster-board. On the due date Teacher V asks for volunteers, who then explain to the class the concept and how it works, using the poster-montage to illustrate. Each student answers questions raised by the class and the teacher. How could you change the strategy to increase problem-orientation?

PART II
WHY THE SYSTEM FAILS

11

Reform of Education, TV, and Public Policy

Periodically, American education is assailed by a wave of protest and cries for reform. We hear that the system is not functioning, the students and graduates ignorant and averse to learning, the bureaucracy swollen and rigidified, and the results of teaching minimal, even counterproductive. There is a certain truth to some of the complaints, especially given the knowledge explosion and the ever-growing need for a well-educated citizenry in the modern technological age. But then too, the schools are beset by social and economic problems not of their own making. Both the schools and the students reflect the larger society.

What everyone seems to forget is that similar cries for educational reform have been repeated almost every decade and certainly every generation. Older people always have found a great lack in the young, while conveniently becoming narcoleptic whenever mention is made of their own foolishness and failings during school and college years. What we adults do tend to remember are nostalgic dreams of challenge and a coming of age. Our time, our age.

The real problem of educational reform is not the failings of youth but how to change the schools so they offer a more relevant and illuminating experience. Schooling should be an opening experience, an introduction to a joyful life of thinking and lifelong romance with education. But many people in education refuse to face this reality and insist on sculpting and measuring education as though school is an end in itself. Many critics and reformers have limited teaching experience or lack current commitment to classroom instruction. They see things dimly from above and through a distorted lens, and I would guess that some could not lead the way out of a paper bag. Thus, many of the "reform" ideas bandied about consist of juggling the machinery, rearranging the order of subjects, issuing pronunciamentos about the terrible state of education, and crying for "a return to basics." This means doing things the way they were done thirty or fifty years ago, when, supposedly, everyone was properly educated and learned to think. But the schools have never left teaching "the basics"—and they do about as mediocre a job at it today as they did in the past.

Creative education remains an elusive and little supported value in American society, which reserves its main rewards to the commercial sector. That most people think they were well-educated in school is tribute to the poverty of critical thinking both then and now. We will probe for answers to these dilemmas in our final essays.

As things now operate, education is segmented and flat. The universities blame the secondary schools for poor preparation; the secondary schools blame the elementary, which, in turn, blame the parents; the latter return the compliment by blaming both the teachers and the schools. Television and movies, drugs, language problems, the economy etc. become valid disclaimers of guilt for all concerned. Every party is right to some extent, and everyone thus escapes responsibility for taking the lead in reforming strategy. That might require working together, demanding intelligent leadership, and getting rid of phony concepts of status and place. It would certainly also require a hard look at TV.

Television has become the biggest challenge to books and schooling. Although TV can lay claim to important educational virtues (presentation of science, and public interest programs, and perhaps the "news"—although that too has become a sideshow with snippets of movie life, car chases, cops, the stock market, glamour, gossip and glitz)—by and large it has become a distraction from serious thought. All too commonly, TV and films offer children and adult consumers a bill of fare that is heavily weighted toward the peripheral, the unseemly, the violent. It has become the popular medium for the quick fix—barren stories, empty characters. Through it runs the cry of the huckster, the relentless search for the easy buck, the omnipresent commercials so cleverly tailored to sell. Tens of millions of young and old are conditioned to watch an endless parade of bad taste and worse art as a daily routine. Television, more than criminals, has made violence as American as cherry pie, by constantly and repeatedly drilling the abusive and sordid into an acceptable part of American home life. TV has been made a profitable habit, an electronic drug that simply cannot be the neutral influence claimed by its producers who are, we must remember, mainly university trained. They too have learned to play the game.

Again, although there are great programs on television, they are the exception and their audience is not huge most of the time. For this, one can rightfully blame not only parents, but the schools and colleges, which have failed to take

TV seriously—at least to the point of teaching young people how to be alert and intelligent consumers of media.

It is argued that the television marketplace is very large and expanding, and that people don't really take TV messages all that seriously. But the growing number of channels is no measure of quality. And advertisers would not spend enormous sums for TV marketing unsuccessful at getting consumers to watch and to buy. The TV sell works all too well, and there lies the problem. Toward what end does it function?—Is the goal really a more educated and intelligent audience? Or, more likely, is it habituating more and more consumers to whoever pays the electronic piper!

A good part of the problem posed by TV is that it fosters passivity. If there is anything the schools (and democracy) do NOT need, it is a passive and unreflective electorate. It is in the realm of spot commercials that TV is most persuasive and does its most deadly work, hammering the populace with claims, mainly false and distorted, in the form of thirty-second sound bites—with little or no opportunity for effective rebuttal.

Because television lends itself to rapidly changing images and short-burst messages, the mindset of an entire generation is corrupted: habituated to roughage, to the avoidance of penetrating inquiry and engagement on the issues. Almost everything is reduced to media-blip, a screamers delight, and the young, impressionable mind is filled with snippets that lack depth and context. There is not sufficient attention span to sustain reflective thought or yield a focus for conducting a long science experiment or anything involving patience. It is akin to what the caustic critic, H.L. Mencken, once said of President Warren G. Harding's wandering "thinking": "His mind is like a colossal Linotype charged with rubber stamps..." It all makes for surface skimming, a facade of knowledge, and the flip authority of the television reporter or politician reading ghost-written lines from a teleprompter.

Whether delivered with a cushioned mallet, a seductive voice and picture, or the hard hammer of the shouter and screamer, visual messages, displayed on either TV or other screens, enter the minds of the viewing audience, often subconsciously, and direct behavior as effectively as a traffic cop. They affect not just choices in the supermarket but choices in politics, style, role, customs and values. Even the best of the worst films tell us how to think and what is "in vogue"—and we fall for it. Too many of us even love it, waiting in wonder and awe for the next set of "cute" commercials. And viewers increasingly identify with the lives of fictional characters, even with their absurd behavior, to the detriment of paying serious attention to what is happening (or not happening) in and to their own lives and that of their community. It's scary!

The negative effects of political spot-advertising on the free marketplace of ideas obviously was not foreseen by James Madison in The Federalist #10, extolling the balancing power of multiple factions of relatively equal influence. As the media have come to dominate and control the marketplace, the influence of powerful, moneyed interests has become almost taken for granted. TV has made the "spots" part of our coat, a "normal" price of modern living.

Add to that a steady diet of violence and nonsense, all destructive of discourse and fawning on sick behavior. Hardly a part of good comedy, it models life inimical to education. Serious dialogue is essential to a meaningful and productive spirit of free men and women. Thankfully, there are uplifting stories on film from the comic to the tragic. We need to get a much larger audience to watch them regularly. But by dominating and drowning out the arenas of debate and reflective thinking, the negative power of TV, to greater or lesser extent, derails and immobilizes the political process and greatly weakens the influence of the schools. We had better begin to think about that.

High School Reform

Everyone is having fun swinging on the educational pendulum. Today the fashionable solution to problems in secondary education is more courses, traditional courses, and a "toughen up," conservative approach to teaching. Witnessing these desperate measures, the educational historian can but smile wryly.

Anyone familiar with educational history knows that the present educational puzzle grew out of the well-documented failure of the traditional curriculum to interest students in subject matter or to give them a grounding in "basic" knowledge and skills. Just look back a half-century or less: The critics of the 1950's decried the "quackery" and intellectual slippage in the public schools that led to a then-growing scientific inferiority, symbolized by the early success of the Russian space program. Commentators in the 1970s, in turn, often looked aghast at the education of the 1960s, which produced both hippies who were uninvolved in their formal education and social activists who were censored for taking theirs too seriously.

Each generation claims, in retrospect, that its own school experience was the "real" education, conveniently forgetting its own educational follies.

Certainly, there is no room for an indulgent attitude toward civic apathy and ignorance. Nor can society ignore any untoward influence of the media in shaping minds and values, especially as this relates to a simultaneous decline in the influence of the schools. In our time of fantastic growth at the frontiers of knowledge, education must clearly change and stay abreast of change. But change toward what? And with what kind of financial support and parental backing? We must remember that even in Japan, where conformity and pressure to perform are national and family traditions, there is growing rebellion against the rote learning system, the dulling pace, and the constant threat of failure imposed by the schools.

A number of myths must be exploded if serious reform of high school education is to take place. I note three recurring fantasies that have led educational reformers down one blind alley after another:

1. Stuffing the turkeys: As we have already seen, this obsessive myth casts students as primary receptacles for discovered truth. The goal of the teacher and the curriculum design is to stuff all the "turkeys" full of facts, then to examine them to insure they are properly crammed; if not, we can set off a new round of wailing about the failures of the schools and our lost generation.

Deep down we all know what an empty and boring ritual is this kind of schooling and examination process. It is true for teachers as well as the vast majority of students. The evidence on lack of retention of subject over even a relatively short run is overwhelming. But somehow we manage to invoke this ancient ritual of cramming as a way of fooling ourselves into thinking that we are "toughening up," that we can wish ourselves back to some imaginary "good old days" when education was Education!

So lip service is given to the gods of curriculum. The problem unresolved by those who would reform education in such a mechanical fashion is that facts are empty when divorced from the critical process by which they were discovered. Remembering lists of names, dates, and facts is but the surface of knowledge. Again, we must refer to Einstein's telling comment that imagination is more important than knowledge.

To invoke and sustain the process of critical thinking calls for highly trained and motivated teachers who know their goals and priorities. And the schools neither attract or retain many of those talented people because in good part the society denigrates and ill-rewards teaching. As my students, who are now parents, used to say, "Put your money where your mouth is."

2. Stretching the rubber band: This myth is that new knowledge and more subjects can be endlessly poured into an inelastic school year. As new subjects (computers being one of the latest) crowd the curriculum, everything else is squeezed tighter or pushed out—especially music, art, and the humanities.

Alternatively, there is the cry to extend the school day and year in order to make room for more subjects. This faulty equation of more with better is like arguing that a weak baseball team can be improved simply by increasing the number of innings in a game. It won't work. The mind is a muscle that thrives on alternate periods of exercise and rest. Better teaching and better learning, like better coaching and better play, cannot arise from dull pedagogy and a fractionalized curriculum, however dazzling the array of subject titles. The cry to extend the school day and year ignores the realities of creative teaching and the common heavy weight of teaching loads. Few school reformers seem to deal with these harsh educational realities, and fewer still are willing to face up to the cross-disciplinary challenges posed by the nature of the modern world. So everything gets squeezed into tight time schedules, and a chopped-up curriculum. As my students, who are now parents, used to say, "What does all THAT have to do with anything?"

3. Running the 18 year dash: This myth is that there is something magical about age 18 that spells "readiness." Readiness for what? The choice is clear: move on to the university or to the "real world." School reformers love to pronounce that learning necessary for citizenship, intellectual awareness, and eco-

nomic progress (i.e.: earning lots of money) will be accomplished, sooner or later, by some favorite version of a high school curriculum. Take your pick: Reading, writing, and trigonometry; the study of alcohol and drug addiction; the Great Books; survival Spanish; income tax and check-book readiness; world history since Adam and Eve (at least two versions); computer programming; auto shop; organic chemistry; wildlife preservation; scientific method and how to avoid getting pregnant; parenting; word processing; European backgrounds and minority contributions to America; football, jogging, and Third World studies etc.

Of course, no one agrees on what constitutes "the basics" or on how they are to be measured, other than by machine-easy scoring of multiple choice tests. And no one seems to ask why student motivation should rise in the face of depersonalizing technology that offers the dreary prospect of a life of endless retraining and re-certifying for a programmed existence of workdays and leisure spent fixated on electronic boxes and screens. The reformers feel that "essential learning" has to be accomplished by the time of high school graduation.

By this standard, many a late bloomer is doomed never to flower, and a great many young skyrockets, despite all the early promise, will nonetheless fall fast and hard in their early twenties and thirties. An opportunity for creative mixing of young people with much older and wiser heads is lost because of the rigidly age-graded curriculum. And education remains segmented, frantic, and wasted—an amalgam of snippets taken out of context. As a long-hardened system, it churns out great numbers of pseudo-intellectuals, anti-intellectual technocrats, and willfully ignorant dropouts in an age that can little afford either the snobbery or the ignorance.

Let's face it: there is no magic curriculum! Nor is high school a sprint to a line drawn in the sand. Secondary education is a gateway to lifelong learning—or it is a blind alley to educational dry rot. It is certainly much more than the opening gun for running laps in the rat race to riches. In high school, there will always be the magic of youth, and there will always be the opportunity to find oneself and one's place in the flow of history, and to sharpen critical thinking skills on many whetstones. High school is but one of many transitions. We need to make the most, not the least of it.

So we must stop thinking of education as a commodity; we must discard the three myths of educational reformers, who mirror a public looking for a quick fix. Instead, we must return again and again to Plutarch's well-considered dictum: "The mind cannot be seen as a pitcher that needs to be filled, but as a flame that must be kindled and fueled."

The School Crisis As a Crisis of Culture

At various times in the school day, you can see them climbing over the school walls or sneaking past the gates to freedom outside. Inside the plant, countless youngsters perform the ritual of high school by the simple expedients of sleep, feigned attention, ritualistic copy work, writing notes to friends, wandering the corridors and bathrooms, and otherwise hiding from teacher imperatives by turning off. Inside and outside the classroom walls, a huge number of our kids are on the loose.

It is both a truism and a cliché that school is a reflection of and on the society at large. The education mess that we all deplore extends far beyond school boundaries and threatens the very foundations of American society and culture. Racial strife, gangs, drugs, apathy, inability to focus on anything beyond the perimeter of immediate gratification, rebellion against authority (and against mechanistic teaching), lack of home dialogue and effective parental guidance, absenteeism, violence, fixation on television and the movies—all are signs of a revolution in behavior and a breakdown in ethics that cannot be fixed by the traditional administration of plumber's tape and chewing gum remedies for sick schools.

There was a time in American history, extending perhaps to the 1970's, when school problems could be smoothed over or adjusted by tampering with various aspects of school operations. In those older times, the dominant middle-class kids and their parents and teachers could be enticed by small reforms and rewards aimed at liberalizing overly tight management; schooling was then by and large accepted as a necessary and routine hurdle race to graduation, college, and the push to a richly rewarded career. Today, despite all the well-intentioned efforts of reformers, the string has run out; big city school's especially cannot be so easily repaired and made long run smooth-functioning by virtue of reformed curriculum guides, tougher courses and discipline, computerization, theme magnets, and nostrums such as "back to basics."

Over the past thirty or more years, these reforms have been tried many times, with sometimes apparent or temporary success. But viewed against the overwhelming problems impacting the schools, they have become small wins in a total war. High school is a literal battleground despite every appearance of calm and order painted on by the presence of security police.

Continuing into the 21st century, secondary school, particularly high school, has become a jumble of conflicting passions and interests. The society has changed dramatically in just one generation. The economic rewards of having more and more formal education are less apparent in an era of layoffs, restructuring, and on-going transformation. The shift to a work-life of transient opportunities offers a shaky future, lacking in real pillars of economic and social security. A worrisome, marginalized underclass is fast developing, with enormous potential costs to our society. Being placed in the custody of school was perhaps tolerable when young people would return to a fairly stable home life with caring and available parents; eventually the young would fly free to a relatively classless and predictable world of work and living, with all its challenges but with also much certainty. It is quite another experience to be abandoned to school as a holding tank and family substitute with very uncertain hopes, financial and otherwise, for the future.

So the gap between young and old, between the youth generation and that of its parents becomes ever wider and looms as a danger to the very fabric of society. "Growing up" in the impersonal and often dangerous world of school today means a much more painful isolation from adult life, care, and opportunities than was true ever before. The kids see through the hollow world in which their parents and guardians live and work; they see how little their elders give time for family life; the shoddy stuff parents watch on television; the marriage to an host of endless deadlines and unfulfilling schedules; the frictions and insecurities of adults and their disquiet and exhaustion. And as Neil Postman has so sharply observed, childhood itself has all but disappeared before the open windows of the mass media.

With TV, computers and school peers as real parents and role models, the whole idea of mom and dad as custodians and surrogates of culture has become a bit of a joke. Those adults who are school teachers are especially imperiled by the shifting economic climate and by the chasm of inter-generational mistrust. This is not even to consider the added burdens to the classroom imposed by waves of migrants, with special needs of diverse cultures and language groups, which stretch and strain the abilities of most teachers and school districts. A single teacher cannot overcome the odds imposed by a large class with such disparate elements. Too frequently the result is chaos.

Clearly something drastic must be done to change the fundamental operation of the system. What the young lack in high school is a key element missing in the plans and goals of education reformers—the opportunity to interact with adults in an adult, but not parental, setting. And certainly not in the dulling stupor that characterizes so many lessons. High school, as we have long known it in America, has become an anachronism. It perpetuates and encourages a teen culture without a transitional-age purpose. As things stand, it tries to teach acceptance of authority in subject, manners, and morals. But the teaching lacks relevance to life, and what comes across is learning how to run hurdles and march in place. High school today still functions more to segregate the young from adults and adulthood than to prepare them for the real world. In this sense it creates the very monster it seeks to destroy: a cult of youth without real responsibility or livelihood, feasting on its own worst tendencies drawn from media image and hype and from marginal or worse surrogates that mirror a lost and silly condition. It is a special world of titillation and vibration, of conformity to passing fads and sounds, and to ultimately boring meandering. In minor key are purposeful, difficult, but also romantic steps that mark a real growing up. The passage of the teen years mirrors the pulse of a society that feeds it with image and an occasional real bone. In three hundred years, our country has moved from rule by divine right of kings to a self-inflicted despotism of the glands

The kids switch off their teachers (and other adults) performing just enough to pass, often shunning those who shine academically. To the extent they have to, they play or pretend to play the school game. In effect, they take over, mimicking the most infantile and deadly aspects of adult life including, most recently, the cult of the gun.

High school as an exclusively teen-age institution must be ended. The way to constructively energize the young is to neutralize the powerful magnet of teen-groupie culture and the gang and snobby social clubs; instead to allow the young to BE adults, but not necessarily to follow in the behavior mold of their own parents. High school must be changed into adult common schools, common in the sense that they are OPEN TO ALL PEOPLE REGARDLESS OF AGE, so long as they have completed middle schooling. In this sense, the traditional separation between adult education and youth education would terminate.

By saturating the new adult common schools with a wide mix of ages, teen dominance would end; the generations would be forced to live with and confront each other on a peer basis, affording opportunities for friendship, guidance, and self-awareness and knowledge. For the teenagers, it will be the long wished for opportunity to be adult—to put up or shut up. For many parents it will present a bootstrap opportunity to do the same.

The new adult common school will offer a full range of courses from morning through evening, with student schedules much more elastic than those found in most high schools today. The curriculum of common school would have work-study opportunities such as are found in almost all community colleges. Students will be measured by product, not just seat time, with emphasis on both faculty and peer review of presentation and portfolio, as is already practiced in some of the best model schools and colleges

Even as teen dominance of the school ends, so too would end college dominance over the curriculum, which warps youth education and is a cause of scandalous drop-out and course-of-study segmentation. It is essential that schools better serve full social and economic and liberal education needs of society and not simply the special interests and peculiarities of college entrance requirements. Even for the college bound, the high school curriculum fails to meet basic civic, parenting, health, and other needs. Health education is subverted by bad nutritional standards on campus and by college recruiting for winning sports teams, which warps the curriculum. And despite all the high-sounding talk about tough entrance requirements, college years are known for considerable remediation, grade-inflation, and artificial prerequisite-course requirements that serve largely to inflate departmental budgets.

We have to stop deluding ourselves about youth and adulthood, about sacred curriculum cows, and an unreal "need" to insulate teen-agers from the world of work and civic dialogue. It is possible to break out of the cycles of violence and indifference, of lost creativity and lost productivity spawned or reinforced in so many high schools today.

The adult common school reform I advocate may not be a universal remedy, but it is a powerful and positive alternative for communities seeking a more basic transformation of the educational system. For those seeking milder solutions that at least have punch, reform options will shortly be discussed in an article about tending the educational garden while putting reformers on hold.

The adult common schools I envisage will become known for concerned citizenship and studies relevant to both work and life. Sparked by challenging internships and productive community service, these schools will focus on neutralizing generational as well as ethnic antagonisms, consciously avoiding the many costs of the garrison school. A more socially aware and inventive generation of producers will result, hopefully developing new employment vistas and a fairer economic climate.

Too many of today's high schools are relics of a bygone age. Some struggle along and a few survive well, but in terms of modern life and needs they constitute a vestigial drag that needs to be expelled. As a reflection of stagnation in our society, high school has devolved to teen-age turf, an infantile world that mocks the coming of age. We must now change our ways of life preparation and take back that turf in the name of sanity and social equilibrium.

Tending the Educational Garden

Plant a carrot. get a carrot, not a brussels sprout. That line from the musical "The Fantasticks" says something about school reform and implementation. Rather than dwelling on past failures or calling for yet another study of secondary schools, it suggests a focus on performance.

We might wish that politicians would quit their haranguing about "promoting basic education and American values" and deliver some seeds for educational improvement that will bear concrete, predictable results. But little so far suggests that they are able or willing to do that. So, as an avid gardener, I will offer some performance criteria suggestive of ways the system can be rather quickly and effectively changed.

We can't be sure that every proposal for reforming schools will bear fruit. Yet, what follows is a number of ideas for school reform that I wish the politicians would mandate. The results would be highly noticeable and would shake up the existing malfunctioning order. I would hope that school principles, teachers, and boards of education would plant some of these ideas on their own. By next school year, the garden would be well on its way to a most interesting and fruitful harvest:

1. At the beginning of each school year, every high school faculty will publish a list of some seven books for required reading. These books will form a part of the curriculum for all students and teachers in that school. The list will not include textbooks, because the aim is to awaken the imagination and form the basis for discussion—not systematically to impart information. Teachers must integrate these books into the curriculum in all subject areas and in any way they see fit and productive. No students may be graduated from high school without a certificate from the school stating he has grasped the ideas in the 28 books read in grades nine through twelve. The list will be printed on the back of every diploma!

2. As a condition of obtaining tenure, new university teachers will spend at least one year teaching in secondary school. The reason for this shocking innovation: Critics claim that high school teachers need to strengthen their subject-area expertise. And university instructors, who are usually strong in subject area, often know very little about how to teach, other than to stand in front of the class and lecture.

Here is an opportunity for both sides to trade ideas and gain significant and needed expertise. High school students and teachers would benefit from the special knowledge imparted by the young university professors. And the latter—learning first hand what kids are ready and willing to learn in high school—are better able to teach students what they need to learn in order to perform well after high school. University instructors will have to learn some things themselves, namely how to foster inquiry, motivate students of greatly varying abilities and maturity levels, and how to encourage active learning rather than the kind of passive acquisition of information that leads to apathy and turn-off. Instructors will be rated and only good ones allowed to remain.

3. Students with reading, writing, and language problems will receive special small-group tutoring by advanced students and community volunteers. The process can begin even before grade 9, and will continue until the student reaches an acceptable level of proficiency. However, no student may formally enter grade 12 without a certificate of proficiency in basic skills. Penalty for schools that violate this guideline: removal of state certification or, at least, a significant reduction of state funding along with a public notice of reprimand. School administrators will bear direct responsibility for maintaining school performance in the basic skills area.

4. An alternate way must be found to identify and recruit individuals who have an innate talent for teaching and a corresponding ability to work well with teen-agers. One way to do this is to empower a panel of education experts similar to a medical board; the panel should include teachers, some students, and others with teacher recruitment experience. The panel's task is to identify and recruit teacher talent by observing demonstration teaching. Once or twice a year, each interested school district would open its recruitment and allow applicants to compete by presenting a superior teaching demonstration on topics assigned on short notice. Successful candidates, who show appropriate education and references, would then be granted an interim teaching credential. The candidate then has two years to complete a professional teaching credential, while working under the guidance of a mentor teacher.

5. Each semester, every school will select an important social issue as the focus of concern. Students and teachers prepare presentations and attend special activities on the theme selected. This might include films, discussions, research papers, plays and guest forums, and laboratory experiments.

6. High school students in grades 11 and 12 will perform at least 200 hours of community service. Agencies and employers will evaluate student performance and attendance, submitting their appraisals to the school. By the time students have graduated, they will have learned marketable skills which can be significant additions to a resume or college application.

7. Newspaper, television, and film projects as well as the fine arts shall form as important a part of school work as standard textbooks. Teachers must demonstrate a record of innovative class-work and assignments in these areas.

8. The science courses and physical education and health must focus their course work and training on studies and activities that have long run and enduring value for adulthood and for knowledge of preventative health and medicine and exercise. Focus should greatly increase on activities such as bicycling, swimming, yoga, hiking, and nutritional food preparation, which are most likely to keep people fit and aware of health needs through the full range of adult years.

9. Observation and limited participation programs in infant and child care should be established in every school to help make young people more aware of the responsibilities associated with parenthood.

You can plant all of these seeds in your school garden today, some whether or not the policymakers in your state or school district include them in their particular reform package. In some cases, implanting such reforms will not be easy; they will require plenty of hoeing, fertilizing, and watering. But they are sure to give many positive results and stir some fascinating discussion.

In Defense of Public Education

The usual strategy of supporters of public education has focused on pleading for funds, on exhorting the legislatures and the taxpayers in the name of fairness and an equitable distribution of revenues. While such efforts are sensible and partially effective, reliance on this kind of defense more often than not proves wholly inadequate.

Under the pressures of state, federal, and local financing uncertainties, even in good economic times, educational investment has a haphazard history. The costs of computer services alone, including maintenance, supply and new purchases can easily drown attempts at budgeting. Add to this such disparate elements as lost investment from teacher drop-out, a growing angry sectarianism, and multi-faceted school problems connected with immigration, television, bussing, family breakdown and poverty, and it is easy to see why public education has become a convenient scapegoat for many parents and politicians.

At the university level, the question, "Knowledge for What?" has become less a central academic concern. The "Get Rich Quick" ethic has turned much of academia into a refined hurdle jumping contest for both students and faculty, with the latter often bragging about how little they have to teach and how much time they spend grubbing for grants. It makes for a field day for special interest booster groups and for private foundation and government bureaucrats acting in the name of public service and support. The practice of curriculum development and reform, educational policy and finance, and particularly the central and critical role of teaching becomes fragmented and even obscure. The public is swamped by misperceptions and misunderstanding of the role of public education in a free society.

Public universities owe a debt to public elementary and secondary education, the principal source of their student supply. And if only in their own defense as the apex of the educational pyramid, the public universities must take a much greater lead in educating their students about the very special place of public education in American history and society. They must awaken their students and the public to the very real crisis in American education. And they better do a better job at this task than they have done to date. Too many graduates of public higher education are negative about government's necessary role in balancing interest groups, and worse, are antithetical to the public education which nourished them. It is a classic case of biting off one's nose to spite one's face…and an interesting and sad commentary on the quality of the education dished out!

There is a relatively painless solution. A course on the great issues of American education should be made central to the general education requirement for graduation at all public colleges and universities. The goal would be to clarify the role of public education and offer historical perspective on educational policy and options. It would also serve to educate future opinion leaders about the importance of a free and critical education and of the part played by the public sector in which they are participating.

What would such a course encompass and how might it function? Certainly, it would be very important to weigh and consider the differences in incentives and goals between the public and private sectors of the economy. The investment value of a library or school could be viewed against the differing worth of a shopping center, a movie, an advertisement, or a gas station. The need for balance in investment in health, education, welfare, and public safety could be examined against the background of recent national and state budget priorities. Some interesting case-studies could be developed and argued. And students would be asked to research and prioritize elements of a budget pie chart. Some major programs could be weighed in terms of their long run investment value, including such interesting possibilities as: The G.I. Bill; nuclear power; cancer research; tobacco subsidies; protection of prime farmland; highway grants; pork-barreling.

The historical rationale and advocacy for expanded public education in the U.S. would be studied. Students would review, for example, the Northwest Ordinances, the Morrill Act, Smith-Hughes legislation, and the arguments about public education put forth by such as Horace Mann, Daniel Webster, John Dewey. Recent debates in the Congress over education aid would add currency to the historical framework.

A comparative look at educational reform would aim at developing a global perspective on education. The students would examine important and oft-perplexing questions having bearing on our own educational dilemmas. I would include the following:

- Why did German education and society in the 1930's fail their most critical test?

- Why have Great Britain and Sweden, as representative examples, made major efforts to democratize schooling and to develop stronger public education as both a social and economic investment strategy?

- What differences in values underlie Japanese and American education, and what are Japanese critics saying about the tightness of their educational system?

The course would delve into the recommendations and rationale of reports recommending reform of American education, some of federal origin and some state and private investigations. The students might ascertain which stemmed from a pooling of thoughts by panels of critics or experts and which were products of actual field investigations. Then students would be asked to draw up their own set of recommendations for secondary and higher education. Indeed, political myths and illusions of educational reformers would form a tantalizing part of the course. And focus would include special interest groups that pressure the curriculum. After watching a video version of the book, *IN SEARCH OF EXCELLENCE*, students could be assigned to applying to education "the lessons from America's best-run companies."

Finally, panels of students and some guest experts would discuss special problems of public education: church-state relations under the Constitution; voucher plans; school bussing; IQ testing; acculturation of immigrants; the challenge of computers, as well as other scenarios for schools of the future.

Opportunities for careers in teaching and public service should inevitably be probed. The course should include guest visits from young and older teachers and from those who have given service to the Peace Corps and Vista.

Flagging support for public education and the public sector demands a rallying strategy. Variations on the above core study course can easily be made, for here I can only suggest the most important kinds of topics and directions. If we are to train wiser policy-makers and managers, the university must face the reality that the most wasteful and dead-end decisions of the recent past forty years—Vietnam; nuclear power; Watergate; awful land-use planning; the continuing environmental crisis; exploitation of children around the world; the armaments burden; financial de-capitalization of third-world countries, to cite a few—were made mainly by the college-trained. Too often they have proven parochial in view, hypnotized by a money ethic, and sadly short of imagination and ethical perspective.

Indeed, these technocrats and managers have little thought of public education as a historical force and a key national investment. Public schools today, and public universities as well, are losing their democratizing and liberalizing role in American society, as the country is tempted and guided into a two-tiered Old World model of education, complete with the mania for entrance exams and technocratic over-specialization. A feudal stagnation will inevitably result from pursuing such a path, with education divided between so-called elite schools for the affluent, and watered-down quasi-vocational schools for the masses. And such will be advertised as a technologically "advanced" program for an advanced society.

If all that is avowed sacred to our free institutions is to be guarded and energized, American public universities must take the lead in educating future opinion leaders in defense of public education and the public sector, and in support of a dynamic reform movement. Then they will set forth by example what it means to be a vital center for criticism and renewal.

Answers to the Teacher Self-Test

1) The purpose of a lesson plan is to set forth clear objectives for a teaching hour and a strategy for reaching them that will get the STUDENTS INVOLVED IN SOLVING ONE OR MORE PROBLEMS. The purpose might also be defined as designing a lesson on paper aimed at sharpening critical thinking and problem-orientation by the class.

2) In handing out or assigning a reading for discussion, the teacher/discussion leader is obligated to give a fair hearing to the author BEFORE allowing or encouraging criticism of the article. In effect, both teacher and students must be able to put themselves in the "shoes" of the author and fairly be able to state his arguments. Critique comes AFTER understanding of the point of view expressed by the author.

3) The teaching lesson that lies in the often frustrating campaign against cigarette smoking is that presentation of facts of themselves is no guarantee of changing people's BEHAVIOR. Facts need to be put in the context of DISCUSSION in order to make the greatest impact, as in programs such as "Weight Watchers," "Alcoholics Anonymous," "Smoke-enders" etc.

4) To make her strategy more effective, Teacher R needs to pose the relevant art problem of the lesson. Instead of telling the students the differences between Renaissance and Medieval art, she could present representative paintings and ask students to figure out what they see in terms of differences in approach, style, meaning etc. She could then build on this base of discovery.

(Note: This question is one of three in this inventory that separates traditional teaching from problem-centered teaching. In the above example, Teacher R, although otherwise using good planning elements, has lost or thrown away a marvelous opportunity for teaching critical thinking.)

5) The best move now of Teacher S is to break the class into small groups, each with its own discussion leader, to work on the problem or reading. Small groups encourage discussion by virtue of their more intimate and relaxed setting. Full class discussion will much more easily flow as an outgrowth of the small group work and reports made to the class by the assigned discussion leaders.

6) Science teacher U has lost a golden opportunity at teaching problem-solving. True science doesn't begin with "right answers". He needed to follow the open-

ing demonstration by puzzling with the class about the action of the bimetallic strip. Teacher U exemplifies a classic case of traditional teaching, with little emphasis on inquiry and the development of hypotheses.

If you missed on this answer as well as question 4, you need to rethink your objectives and strategy and perhaps also your approach to teaching. Are you too focused on what you are doing and not enough on student development???

7) SHOULD the Peace Corps volunteer leave the work he is doing and resign from his two year commitment? (The answer can be phrased in different ways, but the value question must be dominant.)

8) Asking, probing, wondering, questioning, puzzling, analyzing etc. (many possible answers that focus on inquiring).

9) Teachers with eye contact (and discussion-prompting) problems tend to look directly at the one student responding, rather than searching the faces of all the students to encourage full class participation. This is a carryover from habits of polite conversation, where direct eye contact is encouraged.

10) As each montage is shown to the class, the volunteer ASKS the other students to first try to figure out what concept is being presented.

12

Critical Consciousness and Lifelong Learning

The democratic vision of a community with long-term common interests and ideals, of a legacy to future generations, and of a civilization bettering itself through serious and vibrant dialogue has to a great extent become lost in the one-way streets of the spot commercial, the "me-generation," and the miasma of special and moneyed interests. The educational system too has become prey to these warping influences. Some observers say it contributes fully to the aimlessness.

Education needs to reform, if only to create an essential balance that yields life perspective. Young and old have much to learn and to teach through candid discussion of critical issues and values, focusing on both personal and planetary priorities. Sharpened judgment and the critical mind are essential for both political sagacity and personal growth.

For the past fifty years, voter studies reveal that even among the well-educated, political perception is often vague and disjointed, unconnected to societal values and personal life. Democratic values are commonly reduced to clichés, and image is almost routinely substituted for issues.

The American tragedy—of people on the make, endlessly in motion but often going nowhere—was foreseen by Theodore Dreiser in his 1900 novel, SISTER CARRIE. In its modern form, this tragedy is daily played out in the ever more frantic search for instant popularity and riches, in the titillations of the TV, movie, and computer game scene, and in the proliferation of education hucksters, who show paltry concern for human verities or global issues; instead, they deal in passing fashions that sell, and in the superficial acquisition of discrete skills—the self-help curriculum, so-called.

What we have today is NOT the "learning society." A more apt title is the "forgetting society," one that forgets both historical lessons and the concept of planetary stewardship.

Education is far more intent today on teaching the pursuit of private gain than on teaching the importance of public obligation and the art of democratic dialogue. Much is lost or passed over in our narrow, departmentalized corridors; instead of penetrating inquiry, we get quick surveys, pedantic outlines, short-term recall and ultimate myopia. Students jump the required hurdles—and forget. So do their teachers.

The educational ladder doesn't reach as high because of a general turning toward the lowest and meanest definitions of the education experience. Of course, there are exceptions, but these do not erase a critical need for emphasis on problem-centered education at all levels—primary school through the university.

Rather than offering a curriculum centered on inquiry and lifelong learning, our schools and colleges are governed by a turnstile mentality—shekels for credits and the mass production of rocking chair consumers. We must teach our students to be much wiser consumers of education. They must learn how to choose what is best for their humanity and for their citizenship, and how to strike a balance between those fundamental areas and their purely recreational and vocational interests. This means more dialogue, more emphasis on global issues and value questions, more reflective thinking in the classroom, and much less time spent in passive activities and in skimming textbooks. They must also learn how to appraise films and the media and separate the gold from the avalanche of dross that daily assaults us in movies and TV. These changes will revitalize both education and public discourse, creating a real learning society.

Age segregation in education aggravates the compartmentalized and blocked communication so evident in modern society—large and small isolation from the potentially dynamic marketplace. Tragically, these have become accepted in modern urban society as a normal part of living. Out of touch are city dweller and suburbanite, worker and manager, homeowner and apartment dweller, this ethnic group and that, rich and poor, teenager and parents, even husband and wife. All have lost contact and sense of the other, and in the process are lost in themselves, and certainly from the world outside their material interests. To very many people today, the goal in life is to strike it rich, stop the world—and get off!

The focus of real educational reform must sharpen on developing linkage between political and social concerns, and personal problems and perceptions. As Campbell and associates discovered in the course of ten years of study of the American voter, only a tiny minority of politically sophisticated citizens see the connection between personal problems and larger social and economic issues. Despite the daily barrage of "news," the public remains tuned out and fails to grasp events in context. The low amount of information possessed by most people means that most decide political preferences on the basis of simple slogans, catchwords, and perhaps today the meanderings of talk radio. Or news might be ignored altogether so the individual won't become dissatisfied with personal conditions of life.

Age-mixing in both higher and secondary education, and in work, can penetrate some of these barriers and remove a number of blinders. But a meaningful education cannot blossom by passive absorption of collected facts; nor by simply having people of differing ages sitting quietly next to each other. If there is to be real engagement of the generations and the development of political consciousness, there must be a mutual exchange of ideas. This crucial experience only comes to fruition in the course of careful probing of problems and cases that reflect basic political, psychological, and social and economic concerns that often transcend the generations. Inevitably, in work-life as in courses, these revolve around planetary issues and questions of values.

True competence involves taking charge of one's life and awakening to the pressures for conformity and the need to resist by being your own person. That means being free to think and to change; taking the long view of one's ultimate time on the planet; and being willing and able to explore beyond narrow work and technocratic boundaries.

More and more, education seems to go in the opposite direction. Assessments of worth and competence are measured by standardized test scores which are little concerned with values and ethics. Yet, most of the difficulties that arise from "well-educated" professionals derives not from lack of competence but from lack of caring and a shyness about speaking truth to power. True measures of competence, by contrast, always must include some concept of both economic and political ethics, for there is no necessary or automatic link between formal education as it exists—and caring. And without a truly dedicated professional with solid values, there is not even a meaningful link between education and technical competence.

Those who doubt the validity of this conclusion would do well to ponder the breakdown of the criminal justice system despite a virtual tidal wave of new lawyers and police, the malfunction of the schools, the gross inadequacies and unfairness of the health care and welfare system, the diseconomy and dangers of nuclear power, and many special system breakdowns such as the incredible pollution of our ground waters by the chemical additive to gasoline, MTBE.

The evidence of long trained but bumbling professionals and technocrats is today quite evident. Technological progress is grossly hindered by ignorance, lack of caring, short sightedness, and a fool's arrogance. These point to a dire need for basic changes in the goals, methods, and priorities of education. There is simply too little imaginative thinking and too much avoidance of central value questions..

Adult education is commonly adrift in faddism. Amongst the entrepreneurs at countless "learning centers," profits and quick-fix topics are the main curriculum. Less and less is there programmatic concern or student interest in long run issues of vast importance to grown men and women: What kind of world will be pass on to the next generation? What is the meaning of growing older, and how can we make quality use of the years ahead? How can social and economic conditions be improved? What is the nature of the psychological and political forces that affect our self-concept, our values and ideals. How can we create the kind of conditions that yield real security and ecological balance for ourselves and our planet? etc. Such questions yield an important and highly relevant curriculum, one that liberates humans from the obsessions and compulsions of work and play. They are a millennial jump away from the kinds of questions and courses signaling the escapism of the profitable self-help curriculum, with its quest for eternal youth, popularity and riches. Responding tongue-in-cheek to such course titles as: "Lover Shopping at Bloomingdales"; "Facing Up to Wrinkles"; "Cocktails and Computers"; and "How to Marry Money," John Ohliger creates his own list of imagined titles for aggressive adult educators: "Guilt Without Sex"; "Mandatory Education for Parakeet Owners"; "Convert Your Family Room Into a Garage"; "Repair and Maintenance of Virginity"....

Many of the adult education offerings under the rubric of vocational and recreational learning satisfy genuine personal needs. Nonetheless, lacking the benefits of meaningful dialogue to learners and society, a question of balance must be faced. Lifelong learning is a concept only partly related to work and to sport. It includes a major time commitment for involvement with questions that go to the deeper and higher ends and values of the human experience.

As Mortimer Adler made the case for adult education in a seminal paper at Harvard University, we need to educate ourselves "not in order to learn how to earn a living, but in order to use the life for which we are going to earn a living—to learn how to occupy ourselves humanely, to live our leisure hours well and not to play them all away, or seek to amuse ourselves to the point of distraction and boredom. We need to learn how to do well what we are called upon to do as moral and political agents, and to do well what we must do for the cultivation of our own minds."

Hartley Gratton's historical assessment of the development of adult education (*IN QUEST OF KNOWLEDGE*) has become prophetic:

"Adult education has thus far done its best job in promoting expertness and efficiency in vocations, its least remarkable job in cultivating wisdom in the management of public and private affairs. It is now painfully obvious, however, that until we bring our interest and concern for wisdom at least to equality with our concern for vocational skill, we run the risk of catastrophic disaster at some unidentifiable moment in the future."

Even among the better-educated, political perception is myopic, and often only vaguely connected to personal life and the value of preventative action. Yet, political analysts recognize that education remains the single most important factor affecting reception of political information, and even in motivating political activity. Educated people derive satisfaction from finding insights, and this motivates many of them to seek further. They are more likely to know what is happening on national and world stages, but not necessarily to exhibit sophisticated analysis and make sharp political judgments.

The danger, as seen by Tocqueville more than two centuries ago, is that the American electorate can slide into a state of political dissociation and apathy, wherein government policies and priorities are viewed as meaningless and democratic values are reduced to clichés. Recent elections, with their low voter turnouts and mock duels via spot commercials well illustrate this worrisome risk.

Pouring into young and old more of the same kind of education that has not sharpened perception up to now is neither practical nor wise. Each generation tries to avoid real education issues and reform by insisting that what they received was far better than that given to the current generation in school. The truth is that politics and the true condition of the world, both now and before, rarely has been made personally meaningful in the course of long years in schools. The need is not for turning back to "old time education," but for a change in the quality and direction of the total educational experience.

Classroom integration of younger and older students can boost the possibilities of democratic dialogue if dialogue itself becomes a highly valued end, and if the aim of education becomes moral and ethical as well as technical. A truly intergenerational dialogue in turn can create a community spirit and greater consensus; also a greater appreciation of the importance of candid communication, the richness of diversity, and a planetary view. At present, the public lacks the information and curiosity necessary for informed judgment, and has much too narrow training experience in the problem-centered practices to yield historical perspective and a worldview. Other countries share the same restrictive educational patterns—and outlook, many much worse than our own, but this is no reason for smugness.

To civilize the dialogue and make it personally meaningful and fulfilling, the education of adults must also become both less formalistic and less frivolous. A balanced and alive curriculum must center on the great issues—psychological, ecological, and societal—to which students of all ages can and must relate. The trade in free and pointed discussion between young and old, between workers and managers, between teachers and administrators, between family members and among neighbors, leads not simply to interesting banter, but to sharpened judgment and greater mutual respect. That spins off into a richer and more productive society, one which understands the energy and potential of youth and the importance and wisdom of age and community.

13

Quandaries and Readiness

A Tale of Double Vision: Cochise Jackson's Dilemma

When Cochise Jackson's turn came to speak of teacher challenges and dilemmas to the joint seminar of university teaching assistants and student teachers, a bemused quiet took hold. He was undoubtedly one of the class favorites, and always good for a humorous yarn or telling story. He had a way with words and a way with kids, and, as a success story out of the black ghetto, he knew instinctively how to take the measure of a situation and how to take command. He knew the lingo of the streets and was at home both there and in the university setting. Cochise was one of the small group of older student teachers and assistants who had come into teaching through some back door, an entrance that engendered rumors long since embellished and impossible to wipe away. His gangling frame gave testimony to a basketball career long since abandoned, and when he rose and ambled to the lectern there was a murmur of respect mixed in with the ripples of good humor.

"Gentlemen…uh, ladies too in these days of equality for all people, I have been asked to reflect with you on some recent teaching experiences…and, I suppose, to tell a few "war stories" to get you to thinking critically. We all love war stories, because we all want to find heroes, I s'ppose. That must tell us something about ourselves…but I haven't yet figured out what. Maybe we can figure it out together. Maybe not." Jackson looked at the assembled group of new teachers, master teachers, and professors, and smiled. He waited a few moments for his remarks to penetrate past the ruffles of laughter.

"Now all you pale faces out there, pay especial attention to the first of my stories. That don't mean you darker people can go to sleep, no way. But it do mean (Cochise knew the correct grammar but he also knew how to play for effect) that we might get some differing views on my two teaching stories based on your own particular cultural background. It will be interesting to see.

Now, as some of you that knows me know, I have what is called a double assignment in student teaching. I took this not just because I love to work double, but so I can graduate this June. One might say that I is a racing fool—racing to get out the door and into the *real world* where a man, or woman, gets paid real wages, if not much, for teaching. Anyway, I teach mornings at Carver Junior in the ghetto. And afternoons, I race out to the plushy Oakwood Knolls suburbs to teach at Luther Burbank Senior High. You all remember Mr. Luther Burbank as the man with the green thumb. Green! That's kind of funny, cause the school is lily white except for a smattering of bus-ins. So, depending on the time of day it is, I see the world as black or white. But how do the world see me?" Another wave of laughter rolled through the audience as Cochise Jackson played with his glasses and threw a bemused look.

"You see, you are looking at a man with dual vision. Double vision, some might say. And double vision makes the world blurry. So I'm going to ask for your help in seeing clear after I tell you my stories. And here goes. One day last week, I think Wednesday, I decide to give my 9th grade social studies class at Carver some writing experience with a real life situation. So I got hold of a bundle of job application forms from an employment agency that switched to a new format.

I set the stage for the class with some personal stories about the importance of getting a good job. We bantered about different career possibilities, including summer and part time jobs. I then stressed the importance of job application and forms and had a student write on the blackboard these words: neatness; legibility; presentation; ability to follow directions. I had the class respond to some simple questions on lined 3 x 5 cards to practice, before I passed out the 2-page job application forms. Then my idea was to have them make up a career choice of their interest and fill out the form as if they were qualified to meet it. They could choose a simple job appropriate to their age level or could choose an advanced career.

I gave them a few minutes to begin and then I slowly began to move through the class giving advice and suggestions. It was then that I noticed that one student was sitting with her arms folded and was not doing the assignment. I went over and spoke to her. "Lucinda, my friend, why are you not doing your work?" I thought she might have been sick or simply didn't understand the directions, although I was puzzled because she is one of the sharper students. "Mr. Jackson," she says to me with those big eyes of hers, "really, I'm not filling out no such form. I'm going to be a momma in a few years."

"Are you kidding me, lady," I ask her quietly. (No, she is dead serious.) My mind is dazzled and races. A "momma," for those of you who don't know, is someone who has kids as a way of getting on welfare. Hardly a great investment for a bright young girl with lots of college potential. Is this the teachable moment? I decide that it is. I'll risk it. I talk quietly with her a few moments and clear the way.

"Hey class, hold up what you're doing a minute. I have an important point to discuss and I'd like your advice and opinion. Lucinda, is it o.k. if we try to think this through together?" She readily assents and is glad for the attention. "Lucinda thinks that its a waste of time to go about filling out job applications. Most people don't make it out of the ghetto, I suppose, and Lucinda feels that the easy way is to have kids, get on welfare, and become a momma. Now, how do the rest of you see that? Well, to make the lesson for us short and clear, more than half of the class agreed with her and were able to argue persuasively in her behalf. I think I turned a lot of them around, probably because I'm older and wiser and argue better. But I have to tell you that I was demoralized and wiped out by the experience. The problems in central city are overwhelming. And even I, who am a product of that environment, tend to forget this. So much for my first story. Put it in your right eye, while I fill up your left with my very next day experience at Burbank Senior.

On Thursday, I drove out to the Oakwood Knolls armed with a neat exercise I put together in critical thinking. The class was working on the industrial revolution, and after a review of background and terms, I handed out copies of the lyrics to the musical, Mary Poppins. You may remember the particular song that described the merry life of the chimney sweeps of industrial England. We read along with the tape recorded lyrics that described how the young boys happily kept the industrial revolution moving by cleaning the soot from the factory and home chimneys. Then I had my 9th graders write down some adjectives that would best describe the job of chimney sweep, from the evidence and description given in the song. By and large, they reported the work in a positive light. At this point, I handed out a short poem titled, "The Chimney Sweep," by William Blake. Contradictory to the description given in the song lyrics, the poem described in gripping terms the horrible working conditions and the terrible shortened lives of these young boys, who were taken advantage of by the demands of the new industrial system.

"Now," based on the accounts before you, which is probably more believable and more accurate?" I looked around the roomful of middle class kids. Several students had their heads on their desks, a number were obviously daydreaming or looking out the window. Several girls had mirrors on their books and two of these were combing their hair. In fairness, there were the usual eager five or six students with their hands in the air. I decided to probe amongst the less interested.

"Jeannie," I called, "and the rest of you 'hair people', if you would comb and speak at the same time, which of these descriptions of life in industrial England seems more on target? Come on," I urged, "y'all got some good heads on those shoulders." They looked at me half-amused and a lot bored. "Really, Mr. Jackson," Jeannie finally answered, I'm not much interested in past history. Couldn't we discuss something more current like the drug problem or something?" Everyone laughed. I got the class back on track with some comments about how we can learn from the past and that problems today often reflect problems from other times. I also made a pitch on the importance of assessing evidence, but deep down I knew that maybe only 50 percent of those kids showed real interest in the lesson. Ah, many a truth is said in jest, I thought. Supposing we were discussing a current problem such as the homeless people or the lack of good jobs in minority areas. I doubt that would arouse much interest in Oakwood Knolls. Let's face it, the "me generation" of rich and poor wants mainly to be entertained. Our kids like their parents seek a quick fix. I do what I can, the best I can, but something is missing....

So these are my war stories of last week. And now I ask you here, my peers and teachers, which of these two groups, one from the ghetto and one from the suburbs, is most damaged by segregation? Why do we think we are protecting kids by isolating them or teaching them lists of key names, dates, and ideas in formulas for instant recognition—but without understanding or compassion. Has a long history of bad education driven out demand for the good? These are the questions I went home with last week that caused my blurred, bi-polar vision. So I want you to help me clarify my thinking...How can we improve education in these two communities? How can I become a more effective teacher? What about you? Are we all casting stones at the sea?"

Cochise Jackson raised his eyebrow quizzically, smiled, and waited for a response.

Discussion: Here you should be able to write 10-12 good discussion questions on the meaning and implications of Jackson's challenge and dilemma:

Lamenting Teacher Training

Bemoaning the state of teacher training by schools of education has become almost an academic ritual. As the influence of the humanities and social sciences declines, and the power of university business, computer, engineering and technology departments increases, the temptation is to make schools of education scapegoats for failure or neglect of general education. Teachers at primary and secondary levels, and particularly their training schools, are blamed for a host of ills ranging from illiteracy to lack of adequate preparation in core subjects.

In fact, teacher candidates are trained by university subject departments, and claims of subject matter insufficiency should be referred to the appropriate window. Candidates for a teaching credential mainly enter the training process late in their candidacy for an undergraduate degree, and sometimes not until that degree is attained with a subject major and minor in hand. Even more to the point (however puzzling), there is no inevitable connection between high grades in college and strong ability to teach a class. Communicative skills and even charisma here enter the picture..

The mounting problems faced in today's schools call for more and different professional preparation. It is illogical to insinuate that less training in education will yield better teachers. Applied across the board at the university, that faulty argument would shake loose more skeletons than could be found in all the education department closets in the nation. For example, it would require that we explain why the medical schools and their graduates are so ill-equipped to function in the areas of nutrition and preventative care; why research reveals profound ignorance of American voters who have been long exposed to compulsory courses in civics and history; why the justice system has broken down despite (or because of) an abundance of law school and police graduates; and why business M.B.A.'s have led the way in eroding America's manufacturing base and have failed to prioritize environmental benefits or assess true pollution costs. Finding the answers to such important issues would be more fruitful and interesting than poking at schools of education.

Teaching is not as simple as some critics claim, especially those who think that anyone who attended college for four or more years is automatically fit to teach. Teachers often face captive audiences of learners straining to find themselves and their place in a fast changing world. To succeed in the classroom, a developed sense of motivational strategy and communication skill is as vital as a grasp of subject content. But role models in the university especially are not commonly learner-directed.

College student days are too frequently passive, listening to lectures and rehearsing their notes. The creative spark, learning to draw inferences and arrive at original conclusions is a bit of an oddity. As they watch professors dance or trudge through the hour, students become conditioned to a learning pattern that is not encouraged in the best schools and in models of business excellence. Indeed, many "teachers" in university departments openly avow this to be true; they were hired as researchers and grant seekers, and are assigned a class or two as a form of obeisance to academe and the state. Doubtless, some teach well; others are too pompous and pedantic to motivate or inspire young learners.

Education departments have their share of pretentious pedants, but these afflict other departments and are found in all organizations. They only further underscore the need to attract real talent and to give strong support to teaching and training both in the university and in public schools.

While the public and the politicians loudly proclaim the need for educational quality, teacher salaries are still far too low to attract and hold the best talent; with housing costs skyrocketing, teachers, like other professional talent, are being edged out of the possibilities for a middle-class life, and this despite all their years of education and training. School districts are thus drawn to recruit the minimally trained to insure a live body in front of every class so the shekels keep rolling in from the state. Mechanistic teaching plans are the order of the day, part of a move away from creative teaching that sharpens critical thinking skills needed for success in the modern world.

While recruiters scurry to fill the growing number of empty slots at the entry levels of teaching, school systems are hemorrhaging from the loss of mature and well-trained teachers with strong experience. Ten crack armies of educators could be fielded today with the personnel that have been pressed to silently withdraw from the profession. The poverty of teacher salaries is matched by the poverty of personnel policy, and exodus is the result. Teaching and education administration have become virtually separate worlds with different concepts of reality and different illusions as well. The typical big-city administrative bureaucracy is overblown, grossly overstaffed, filled with deadwood, and unable to face the realization that it exists mainly as a service arm for the teacher and the schools. To a slightly lesser degree, the same could be said about the exploding bureaucracies at universities, which so identify with the corporate model and corporate aims and values. The ever-frantic search for contracts and status based on moneyed success is alarming; the corruption of values and the accompanying denigration of teaching is tragic.

Yet, through it all a few good men and women, here and there, in this department or school or that, keep the educational ship afloat. Our educational system, although badly shaken and sometimes way off course, beset by added problems of family breakdown, negative media influences, and the burdens imposed by waves of immigration and by seductive and non-intellectual alternative life styles, is still viewed with envy by reformers in other nations. Critics may scoff at American schools and point to elitist models abroad and in the expensive and self-selective private sector. But the truth is found in comparative studies matching like to like; these show that our high performing public school children to be roughly equal to their counterparts in highly selective school system here and abroad. The challenges (and burdens) of mass education need yet to be tested fully in Europe and Asia, while the rewards of a more open system here have led educators the world over to question class biases and lost talent in their own schools.

Undoubtedly, major changes are needed as I have suggested throughout this book, including basic reform of teaching itself and in the status it enjoys in the society and the university. Continuing into the present, education is not accorded the same academic recognition and university support as cattle raising, computers, business and advertising, and a number of other high income producing specialties. That says more about misplaced university priorities than about education potential. The goal of every subject department in higher education should be to spin off an increasing number of its graduates into teaching careers and to do this in both word and deed, using models of excellence and promotion of the teaching arts.

So, we must ask whether the university is serious about coming to the aid of the besieged public schools? Some are and show it with serious cooperative efforts. Perhaps the answer would be much easier if education coffers were as full as those prompted by tax loopholes for multi-national corporations.

I do not plead for special privileges for education, but simply for fairness and balance. There lies latent much potential for improving university teaching and learning. It is long time overdue to end the phony campus war over status and place.

When the Very Young Teach Us

He was six years of-age at most and maybe three and a half feet tall. He stood on the plateau at Mesa Verde National Park like an immovable and polished boulder, his hands on his hips and his blonde hair blowing in the wind. The lad was determined to go it alone.

"But don't you want to wait fifteen minutes and then we can all go with the park ranger?" his parents begged. The ranger will have so many interesting things to show us and many points to explain."

"No!" came the reply. We can see most of these things for ourselves. And besides, we don't have to go in a crowd."

"True, I suppose," said his mother, "but we've not been here before. We could miss some important things."

"We'll use a map, just like we did in New Mexico," the boy insisted. We'll see the major sites and we can explore the side trails. Don't be so worried. It's fun going by ourselves."

From a prior conversation I had overheard, I knew they had driven up from El Morro and Bandalier monuments, which are much smaller than Mesa Verde; they had doubtless followed the numbered signs to catch the views from the top of El Morro and to explore the caves at Bandalier. The sun rose higher and the morning cool was fast disappearing. Like a horse pawing the ground, anxious to get started before the heat of day, the lad scratched with some sticks tracing the outlines of shadows from nearby boulders.

His dad scowled. The waiting crowd had grown by the minute and now numbered close to thirty people. More stragglers arrived. Dad smiled. "I have an idea. We could go with the ranger for an hour or so. Then we could do an exploratory hike on our own after lunch. The group is almost ready to get started. So what do you say, we wait?"

"No way. Afternoon gets hot and then we won't explore much. We get tired after lunch and everyone wants to take it easy. NOW'S the time to explore!"

The ranger gives us all the details and answers all our questions," suggested mom.

"It's better to see a few things we can remember," retorted the boy. "If we drag along listening to everything he shows us, we end up getting them all mixed up."

"That's often true," admitted mom. "But how can you be so sure we won't miss something special?" Even as she spoke, she winked and nodded to her husband. The boy and his parents broke from the waiting group and began hiking up the trail.

The lad began to skip and laugh. "Well, it can't be that important if it's not on the map and guide. And even if it is, we might find things we like even better."

By now, I could just catch his trailing comment: "Sure I like to talk to the rangers and go to the campfires. But on the trail, they keep explaining everything. They don't let you discover anything by yourself."

14

At the Core of Higher Education

I long remember the brilliant and dynamic Peace Corps volunteer, who, at mid-semester, left a prestigious graduate school and a Woodrow Wilson fellowship to get his real university education. Sick of the pettiness and irrelevance of many of his graduate courses, the incident that sent him on his way to an assignment in Africa was his refusal to indulge in the travesty of an "objective" test on <u>Paradise Lost</u>, given by one of America's famous literary critics.

"He scowled at me, at my offer to take any thoughtful challenge, oral or written, on Milton's work. "I have no time to grade essays," he kept repeating. "It's a large class and my graduate assistants are tied up with several research projects of mine. This is a university, you know, and not a high school. 'The volunteer smiled wryly. In the language of the university, "I dropped out."

Educational institutions either spark a vital marketplace for the exchange of ideas and the sharpening of judgment or they fail as carriers of the democratic vision. When they do fail, they lose their critical uniqueness—the perspective that differentiates them from other large institutions such as banks, supermarkets, advertising companies or factories. The university in a free society simply cannot afford to compete on the same plane as agents in search of a popular market; it cannot act vitally when it becomes a mere feeder agent to the idols of the economic marketplace and consumerism.

We must practice more what we so often preach in academe—to civilize our education and our public dialogue. That is the measure of our ability and will to guide the destiny of a free people—to bequeath the legacy of rational discourse to the next generation. In probing the issues of curriculum obsolescence in higher education, Robert Maynard Hutchins stated the goal as well as anyone: "The political community arises when the citizens are learning to govern themselves…The democratic vision is that all the people are engaged in argument about the good of the community and the methods of achieving it."

Dialogue is the key. If it is to be enhanced through education, it must feed on meaningful content. To paraphrase James Madison, dialogue is to education what air is to fire and what liberty is to faction. An education not tied to intensive dialogue has but the form and not the substance of civilizing exchange.

Because teaching and administration are poorly thought through and not really reformed, the lines of communication on campus remain weak. Dialogue tends toward monologue, and administration sinks to accounting, dictation and public relations. The bean counters are in charge.

Institutions of higher education often view adults as compensatory learners making up for lost time. The great dialogical advantages to be gained as more and more adults enter or re-enter the university are ignored. Conveniently forgotten are the perspectives and learning gained by adults as a result of years of life experience. In lecture-dominated classes, the really creative contributions that adults can make to educational dialogue are lost. The legacy of age segregation, with its child-like stress on filling empty baskets of the mind with an endless stream of facts thrown by experts remains very strong.

As one young student commented, "I feel the older students in class enrich the learning environment. They are more experienced and perceptive and valuable contributors to class discussion. They have a broader view of work, society, life, and they want to share their views, which affects all of us younger people." Another young student stressed the importance of diversity: "A college should allow for a wide variety of thoughts and concerns. The presence of older people in class only enhances learning. Besides, we have to keep the older people young."

Even given a warm acceptance of adult learners into university classes, there remains a growing need for more problem-centered education with its emphasis on discussion and focus on central issues and core values of society. More liberal education, not less, is the hope of any higher education fostering sharpened judgment and critical analysis. Without this focus, even in technical fields, the spark for dialogue is lost and education drifts toward the passive and the peripheral; questioning becomes mechanistic and dull. Thus the key to true educational reform is also a path to unlocking stodgy patterns of teaching, especially at the university, where, all too commonly, high status is accorded those able to brag about how seldom they are assigned classroom teaching duties.

The necessity of university reform requires moving teaching and research out of their traditional isolation and into a coordinated and active maturity. Teaching in the reformed university should become a natural activity for all members of the intellectual community—including the students. As part of the contract for a university degree, every student should assume some form of teaching assignment, whether in literacy training, tutoring in technical subjects, teaching English, or other community service that involves motivating young and old to learn. Required hours in a teacher-training laboratory would reinforce instructional abilities. All that helps provide an invaluable mirror for personal and professional development, regardless of the vocational orientation of the student.

Many students will not prove to be great teachers, but that is no better or worse than what already exists in campus life. Through the challenge of a teaching assignment, the student tests his motivation, subject interest and command, and ability to stimulate enthusiasm for learning and intellectual development. And, hopefully, he or she grows to appreciate how vital are the threads of dialogue in which ideas form, spark, and take fire.

The poverty of pedagogy today is partly a function of the mass exodus of the most imaginative students with the highest communication skills into the lucrative world of commerce, industry, and the glamorous professions. The required teaching internship may well serve to attract many highly capable people into the teaching profession, who would not normally even give it a try. If only for a few years of post-graduate assignment, they will help breathe new life into stale corridors; at best, they will enter the profession now or later. Conversely, many of the drones may be dissuaded from becoming teachers or professors, saving generations of students from turn-off and blather.

In accord with the shift in curriculum objectives for reform, lecture courses will be greatly reduced. Perhaps only 15-20 lectures would be required of a professor in any academic year. These would be publicized as important inspirational and informative contributions to the academy, rather than routine class deliveries. They would provide the professor a special time to profess—to expound on research and offer perspective on important issues.

In the reformed university, courses would be built around problems or themes rather than expository textbooks and outline-surveys of an entire field or historical sweep. In this vein, the seminar, the discussion group, the apprentice lab become key. They set the tone of educational activity. Dialogue is focused on case-studies, experiments, and policy questions. The aim is a sharpening of judgment and understanding and a more meaningful grasp of factual information plus heightened sensitivity to what is right, true, and just.

With every member of the academy teaching at least part-time, from key administrators to the youngest freshman, class overloads will greatly lessen. The "need" for bloated university bureaucracies, peopled with their goodly share of farceurs fleeing the rigors of teaching, will greatly diminish. Vital lines of communication between students, faculty, and administrators will be opened even as the intellectual atmosphere of the campus is invigorated. Those who cry that many university students do not respect the ground rules of democratic dialogue seem to forget that the university today rarely sponsors a true dialogue either in its administrative relationships or in the classroom. Committees are all too often influenced by apple-polishers and those seeking an exit from teaching into administration. They are adept mainly at playing the game. However, in fairness, there are many, many exceptions.

Mainly through a basically changed approach to curriculum and teaching, the university can be brought in line with its intellectual purpose. The alternative is a continued trend toward a more technocratic and bureaucratic entity dominated by a market-driven ethic. It will further open up an era of formalized nonsense and drift, perhaps with a few short-term gains, but without real vigor or fulfill-ment—a time without time for vital dialogue, commitment to change, or mean-ingful personal growth.

"My research has had several positive results, the main one being I haven't had to teach in two years."

The Environment of Reform

The movement toward greater public awareness of the environment and ecology has stemmed from universities as well as the media and environmental organizations. But even as the environmental reform wave has gathered momentum, few people on campus have bothered to ponder the implications of an environmental awakening for university education. The challenge to the university posed by ecology is threefold:

1) the requirement of innovative teaching as a function of cross-disciplinary problems;

2) the need for new forms of articulation between traditional subject departments, or, alternatively the substitution of new and more educationally valid cross-disciplinary forms; and 3) the necessity for coordinated research efforts and educational programs that motivate people to action in solving key local and regional environmental problems. Environmental education demands recognition of the interdependence of educational life even as it is affirmed as a condition of planetary life in general.

The nature of our environmental challenge thus calls for a basic questioning and reevaluation of the university's direction, its goals and purpose, and its organization. It is essential to ask (and answer) how the university can reorganize its curriculum to provide all of its students with a range of perspective and the world view essential to grasping and coping with the ecological dilemmas of our times. While higher education has made major strides in environmental program development over the past quarter-century, relatively few students are enrolled in specialized study, and, more important, the overall effect on college graduates is doubtful. The pace of bad urban and rural development, and technological pressures threatening world ecological instability continue almost unabated. Too few college graduates in the U.S. and abroad take an ecological view of the effects of their own business, professional, and personal lives and activities. "Environment" is too often a glittering generality or catchword used to avoid facing some harsh planetary realities that might stand in the way of personal gain and enrichment.

The modern program in environment and conservation must both encourage and reconcile diverse interests: the preparation of research specialists and university professors and teachers; the education of middle-level and higher policy-making personnel in government and in urban, regional, national and international organizations and planning agencies; the development of a consumer awareness;

focus on a long range planetary view by both business, labor and technical degree aspirants, as well as voters in general. The areas of critical importance are likewise diverse: They include problems of water, air, and soil pollution; legal and ethical implications of conflicts over land use; natural resource depletion and recycling; studies of "planned obsolescence"; alternative transportation initiatives and new-city planning; population studies and relevant programs of education; alternative strategies for energy efficiency and for solving the development problems of poorer nations; environmental factors affecting illness (nutrition), tension, and aging etc.

What the university must come to understand in planning curriculum is that every student is evolving as a shaper of the environment. Many graduates will become key decision makers of or affecting environmental policy. The elements of conservation are found in four cross-disciplinary themes: 1) the effect of technology on society and mankind; 2) the nature of the growing crisis of environmental imbalance and the possibilities for correction of negative trends; 3) political, economic, sociological and philosophical dimensions of the relationship between humans and the environment; and 4) education for environmental action: the development of communication and policy-influencing skills. A basic humanistic concern must serve as the thread that binds together the diverse specialists and provides a common focus for exploration and discovery.

In other words, the core of the environmental education curriculum lies not simply in science specialties, but mainly in those areas in which science becomes a springboard for arguing larger questions of public policy. The effective program will build historical perspective on the conservation movement, and sharpen analytical skills through intensive discussion of substantive issues of local, regional, and world import. The dominant motif of a new conservation approach is the value conflicts underlying ecological issues.

As hydrologist Raymond Nace concluded, "In any organized society, decisions about water necessarily are political, not hydrological, because their purposes are for political entities—cities, countries, states, the nation—which exist for people. Decisions require the making of choices among alternative courses of action, and each choice involves certain value assumptions. Different groups of people hold to different values, so each choice would have different effects on different groups…Hydrologists and engineers alone cannot solve water problems; they can solve only hydrological and engineering problems. The same is true of economists and sociologists. They can tell the planner what he has to deal with…and they can evaluate the potential impacts of alternatives, but that is all. The decision process is something else."

But neither is the planner a god, and commonly the planners problems stem from the narrowness of his training in one or the other departmental specialty. Decisions are commonly made under short-run political pressure and with dollar value as the primary element. Almost inevitably the results go awry. And when blamed for the mess that develops, the planner's propensity to avoid confrontation is reinforced. A vicious cycle of conflict-avoidance is implanted.

The university must ready its graduates to avoid the gentlemanly game of "cop-out." It must better prepare its graduates to engage on the issues and become proficient at sustaining a reasoned position. In other words, it must work to end the shortsightedness of subject specialists who are encouraged to dig that more or less comfortable niche, a place to hide from life behind a banner of "Ethics be damned—I look only to the facts and my orders from above. And I try to avoid the public arena."

Nace also sees this dilemma, and finds it reflected in the three basic sins that beset the planners: Blind faith in science and technology, worship of bigness, and arrogance toward the land. He concludes that rational planning demands an amalgam of knowledge: "Preparation of the mixture is the stage at which the planning process commonly breaks down, because the participants are human and tend to listen chiefly to what they understand best or like to hear."

Ecology cannot be separated from the total range of human problems which rebound against each other and often compound and fuse. In this way the direction of life is determined, its nature affected. The common denominator in ecology is man, because humans have become the dominant agent of change in the environment. Through powerful and sometimes devastating actions upon nature, we exert a unique form of logical—or illogical—control. In this sense, environmental education becomes the essence of all meaningful education. The challenge to the university is to make the study of human-environment relations particularly relevant and important to its students and professors.

What we learn about our effect upon the natural world in turn affects our relations with that world—and therefore with ourselves. The state of the art and science of environmental conservation (ecology, stewardship, call it what you will) is thus a real testing ground, a real mirror for mankind. It is perhaps the principal means for assessing the well-being of the university as well as the health and safety of the planet.

APPENDIX

Planning Exercises

Following are five lesson plans drawn from a few fields with which this author and teacher is familiar. It is best that teachers in different subject areas compose plans that fit the particular needs and peculiarities of their field of study. The goal here is to prompt a process of thinking through plans proposed, both in terms of strengths and areas that could be improved. Perhaps different evaluators will have differing opinions on the likely effectiveness of any given plan. We can look at such things as clarity of direction and purpose via the standpoint of the six basic steps for producing a lesson-strategy plan. First, you decide how you would feel if you were given each plan to teach from, having arrived at the school as a new teacher, or a substitute with good experience in the classroom. I'll reserve my own remarks on each of these plans for a final few paragraphs. One final note: The five plans have purposely been placed in a kind of artificial vacuum, disregarding age and ability levels and without reference to prior study, unit planning or any other factors that normally would impinge on lesson preparation. The object is to focus completely on the written planning process, with the assumption that the students have the capabilities and readiness to handle the material. Let's begin:

Teacher A's Plan:

Topic: Were legal rights violated in the Pennsylvania steel strike?

Objective: The students will be able to explain what the steel workers claimed were violations of their labor organizing and Constitutional rights. They will be able to cite pertinent sections of the Bill of Rights and federal laws, as well as offer concrete examples drawn from the film *Strike at Big Steel* (school film-lab 67343s (fictitious reference for illustrative purposes) Students will also be able to explain the steel company management's position and why strike situations are often so difficult to resolve.

Set Stage:	Does anyone know anything about the steel strikes that have taken place in Pennsylvania? Why is steel so important to our economy, and why do you suppose workers within that industry might go on strike? Vocabulary: picket; lockout; secondary boycott; good-faith bargaining, union shop; job exportation
Strategy:	Show film (15 minutes). Students take notes on: Why are the workers striking? What are their demands? What is the reaction of farmers/clergy/non-union workers? How does the company explain its actions? What are their reasons for moving away? Following the film, the class is broken up into three groups, each of which is to summarize both sides of the controversy and come up with the recommendations for a reasonable settlement.
Discussion:	If you were a steelworker, would you join that strike? As a consumer, would you boycott in sympathy? As a member of management, would you negotiate more? Why? If the workers had legitimate grievances, which seemed most important to you? And which to the company?
Evaluation:	As each group reports, their basis for settlement of the strike is recorded on the blackboard. Areas of agreements and disagreements between groups will be noted by the teacher. Note will be made of specific areas mentioned in the Bill of Rights and labor laws as well as stumbling blocks to strike settlement.

Teacher B's Plan:

Topic:	Inventors and industrial revolution.
Objective:	Understanding what the industrial revolution did for invention. Who were some key inventors?
Procedure:	Take class roll. Review chapter 11. Hand out printout of inventors and inventions. Students match inventors with their inventions. (Morse, Whitney, Edison, etc.)
Strategy:	Teacher discusses lives of three famous inventors of the industrial revolution. Students use their textbooks and make the matches of inventors/inventions on the handout. Brief lecture on patent rights, and the importance of industrial change in the American economy.
Discussion:	Who/What are some inventors/inventions today? Why do some people want to invent things? What are the important uses of the wireless telephones and computers?
Evaluation:	The students will write a one hundred word essay on how inventors helped the industrial revolution and vice versa. Teacher grades these for credit.

Teacher C's Plan:

Topic:	What is *organic farming*?
Objective:	Discussion of problems and perspectives on organic farming and controversies arising from pesticide use.
Set Stage:	Here are two carrots (show them). One is grown organically and the other is not. What is the difference?
Strategy:	I explain how vegetables are grown organically as compared to those grown by most farmers using chemical fertilizers and pesticides. Then, I pass out the case of Langan vs. Valicopters (attached) and after giving students 15 minutes to read it, there is a general class discussion. Vocabulary is explained.
Discussion:	organically?
Evaluation:	Students will write a paragraph on whether this was an understandable and excusable error or whether spraying should lead to some kind of fine. Several volunteers will be asked to read their conclusion to the class.
Case:	Langan vs. Valicopter (State of Washington) The Langan family is organically farming in the Yakima Valley. They rely on using only natural fertilizers and pesticides as farming aids, and do not believe in the use of farm chemicals. As *organic farmers*, they are members of the Northwest Organic Food Producers' Association (NOFPA), and thereby must abide by strict directives against using chemical poisons. If the Langans disobey the NOFPA rules, they would automatically lose their certificate as organic farmers. Valicopters is a Washington corporation that aerially applies agricultural pesticides on farms that contract with them. Next to the Langan's land are the Thalheimer's Farms, a customer of Valicopters. One day, Valicopter sprayed the chemical pesticide Thiodan on the Thalheimer farm, but the wind drift causes the spray to settle also on the Langan's crops of tomatoes, garlic, beans, cucumbers, and artichokes.

When Langan's crops were tested for the presence of chemicals, it was found that 1.4 parts per million by weight of Thiodan was on his crops. Food and Drug Administration tolerance limits on tomatoes and beans was the 2.0 parts per million for Thiodan.

The Langan's certificate as organic growers was promptly revoked. They could no longer sell their products as *organic*, and they did not have a contract that would assure them of non-organic commercial sale. The Langans had to pull their entire crop so that the Thiodan would not further contaminate the soil. The Langans sued Valicopters for many thousands of dollars in damages.

Valicopters argued that is was an innocent error, and that NOPFA was erroneously interpreting its own bylaws. They claimed that the accidentally sprayed crops should have been tested *after* they were fully grown, when the spray effect would have been worn off. Besides, they argued, the amount of spray was under the limit set by the FDA.

For its part, NOPFA insisted that it was its duty to all customers to insure a totally organic product is brought to the market under it seal. Their standards are much stricter than that set out for farmers by the government agency. While they sympathized with the Langans, they had no choice but to cancel their permit. Valicopters and the Langans then appealed to the court.

Teacher D's Plan:

What about World War I? Have we forgotten it?

Objective:	Students will learn about the main issues and events of World War I, and will state three incidents between 1914 and 1918.
Set State:	Here are two newspaper headlines of the New York Times in 1914 and 1916. (show them) Teacher gives a short explanation of the incidents surrounding the war and leading to American entry into combat.
Strategy:	Causes of the war (discussion): system of alliances; Austria-Hungary and Serbia; assassination of Franz-Ferdinand; unrestricted submarine warfare and blockade. Lloyd George and Clemenceau.
Discussion:	Which three of President Wilson's 14 Points seem most important? If you lived in those times, would you have sailed on the Lusitania? Would you have been an isolationist? An enlistee in the U.S. army?
Evaluation:	Students respond to questions by recalling the incidents of World War I. Students will get extra credit if they do a book report on THE RED BADGE OF COURAGE.

Teacher E's Plan:

Topic: What is the meaning of *progress*?

Objective: Students will be able to explain quotes by Thoreau and Krutch and apply
                  them to the Hetch Hetchy reservoir plan. They will be able to apply both
                  sides of the argument about *progress*.

Set Stage: On your computer screen are photos of Henry Thoreau and John Muir. What
                  qualities of character stand out in each photo? (Brief biographies of both
                  men have been read the previous day.)

Strategy: On screen (or chalkboard) appears a quote from Thoreau's Harvard Com-
                  mencement address: "This curious world which we inhabit is more wonderful
                  than it is convenient; more beautiful than it is useful; it is more to be admired
                  than to be used."
                  After discussion of whether this is more or less true than in Thoreau's time, a
                  quote of Joseph Wood Krutch is shown: "...the whole concept of exploitation
                  for man's use alone is false...The earth will have been plundered under this
                  form of conservation no matter how scientifically and how far-seeingly
                  accomplished...The thing lacking is the feeling for, or the love of, the natural
                  world of which man is a part." After discussion of the virtues and drawbacks
                  of exploitation of resources, the class will read Mr. Sampson's challenge to
                  the plan for damming the Hetch Hetchy valley in Yosemite National Park.

Discussion: Is the right to visit public property inviolable? Does the Krutch-Thoreau
                  approach stifle progress? How would a committee of "all-around intelligence"
                  operate differently (or would it?) than one composed of engineers? Would
                  their respective conclusions necessarily differ? What does Mr. Sampson
                  mean in saying, "A man cannot dip up any more ocean than the vessel he
                  carries will hold"?

Evaluation: Students will write an essay justifying or attacking the proposal for removal of
                  the Hetch Hetchy dam, showing that they understand *why* progress is a con-
                  troversial issue.

Attached: case of Hetch Hetchy:

Mr. Sampson's Challenge to Hetch Hetchy Dam

Testifying to the U. House Committee on Public Lands in 1908, Mr. A. Sampson, who had worked with the Biological Survey in California, challenged the wisdom of the plan to dam the Hetch Hetchy Valley in Yosemite and turn it into a reservoir for the city of San Francisco:

Mr. Sampson:	...The citizens of the U.S. have just as much right to go into the Hetch Hetchy Valley today as they have to come here to Washington and see the Capitol. If they are excluded from one-half of Yosemite National Park, they have been deprived of property which belongs to them...It is not the intelligent way to find out whether or not other sources of water supply are available...
Mr. Volstead:	How are we going to be able to get that information?
Mr. Sampson:	Why could not Congress appoint a committee of men, not especially engineers, who are simply hypnotized by the appearance of that as a dam site,...men of all-around intelligence and send them out to see....Mr. Muir, who is an expert (about the mountains of America) says that the Great Hetch Hetchy Fall is the most beautiful (waterfall) he has ever seen.
The Chairman:	That would not be in any way affected by the use of the valley as a reservoir.
Mr. Sampson:	Yes it would...Simply going along a trail on the side of a cliff, and having a look at it, does not cut any figure at all. To appreciate a great waterfall or a wonderful valley like this, you have to go there and stay with it. You might just as well be introduced to a person and then pass along without having anything more to say, but if you want to know him, you have to converse with him.
The Chairman:	Sometimes the former experience is the more satisfactory. (laughter)
Mr. Sampson:	That is so. Allow me to make a comment on that....A man cannot dip up any more of the ocean than the vessel he carries will hold. If he has a pint cup, he cannot dip up very much.

Mr. Kahn:	...the city of San Francisco has investigated (all the alternative choices) and finally decided that this was the only one really available, taking into consideration present conditions.
Mr. Sampson:	It is simply the dream of an engineer...When he dreams of paradise, no engineer alive would not think he was building a dam at the foot of the Hetch Hetchy Valley.

Comments on the five sample plans:

A. Teacher A shows a strong problem orientation and wastes no time in drawing learners into a careful hearing and balancing of opposing viewpoints. This teacher asks important questions that force penetration of the problem and clarification of key terms. Essential facts are out on the table, collected and analyzed by the students, who are brought to focus on legal rights and the judgments that the case requires. Teacher A has a clear introduction, and the problems raised by the steel strike are handled well by his strategy: Learners must listen to both sides shown in the film and come up with insights and ideas for problem solutions. Teacher A guides but does not dominate the learning process. Although the time to run this lesson plan may turn out to be more limited than teacher A has available in one class hour, the overall lesson shows sharp planning and fine command of subject and materials.

B. Teacher B needs to rework his plan so there is a major problem and performance objectives set forth for the learners. As things now stand, the lesson largely calls for matching inventors with their inventions, with little or no definition of *industrial revolution.* There is confusion about the period of history to be studied: is it the 1800's to the 1920's or does it extend beyond the industrial revolution into the age of space and information? The first question for discussion deals with current inventors and inventions, which might make a good stage setting for drawing student interest in the question of industrial change. Perhaps a good topic question for the plan might revolve around whether necessity is the mother of inventions or vice versa? The plan as written seems too scattered; with a lecture on patents rights somehow thrown in as filler material just like the supposed review of chapter 11 at the beginning. The learners are rather minimally challenged. It is the teacher who lectures on the lives of famous inventors as well as on patent rights. The second discussion question is important, but there is a lot of confusion and tangents thrown into the plan as written. I am forced to ask, "How could the students be better motivated and involved in the issue of industrial revolution, technological change, and invention?"

C. Teacher C has presented an important case-study problem, but the lesson plan has aspects that detract from its focus. The stated topical question (What is *organic farming?*) calls for a simple factual definition that cannot hold the class' attention for very long. In any case, the teacher quickly gives the answer, without much probing to see if the students can provide the information. However, using the carrots as a stage setting is a good transition to the case study *if* the students are wisely motivated to explore the issue of organic agriculture. The discussion questions listed do not prompt much discussion, calling for more short factual answers than a penetrating inquiry into the major issues of the case. This may signal some laziness at writing questions or a pedantic approach to teaching. Key issues of rights and responsibilities, what constitutes a "scientific judgment", and what is a fair compensation, and the meaning of NOPFA's seal of approval are all overlooked in the discussion section of the plan. However, the evaluation is to the point and the students are positively involved, including giving feedback to the class. There are sound elements in this plan, which need to be better pinpointed and defined so that the excellent case study can be used to maximum advantage.

D. Teacher D needs to greatly sharpen focus on problem solving. There are simply too many topics to offer anything more than a smatter of surface coverage. Indeed, this kind of unfocused lesson plan is all too common, produced by teachers who fail to understand that a plan involves a step-by-step strategy for developing problem orientation and critical thinking, or by teachers who try to get by with a show of topics to be mentioned. It's a skimpy preparation, and teacher D's lack of valid strategy for conducting the lesson is revealing. The first objective is too vague, and the second calls for minimal recall of information. The stage setting has potential, although never clarified, and in any case, the headlines are used only as an opener to teacher exposition. The plan shows little attempt at class involvement. The discussion questions are acceptable, assuming the students are cognizant of the issues. But how can one realistically expect to do justice to World War I in a single teaching hour? The topic is too broad and is not worth the attempt. Teacher D may know much about World War I, but his plan is obtuse and scattered. Aside from the book report option, the plan is lacking creativity.

E. Teacher E presents an ambitious plan notable for its clarity, incisive questioning, fine selection of relevant materials, and imaginative sequencing. Each phase of the written plan unfolds into the next and leads to a challenging evaluation section, which ties beautifully to the stated objectives. Teacher E will need to carefully make the transition from the quotes to the testimony of Mr. Sampson in the Hetch Hetchy case, but given his sharp questioning, he seems likely to do this without losing the discussion in tangents. He might also play devil's advocate for the other (development) side and have the class bring in follow-up arguments on both sides of the resource exploitation issue that can be found in newspaper and magazines. Teacher E stimulates his students to think deeply and penetrate the carefully chosen material. Interest in the subject is stimulated by the use of photographs in the stage setting. Here is a particularly fine example of problem-centered lesson planning, one that shows great concern for critical thinking and meaningful student involvement with well chosen materials.

Looking Back—The Closing Of The American Mind

✦

Allan Bloom's Proclamation

(obiter dictum—Ira Winn)

Descriptions of spiritual and intellectual malaise in America and American education are seductively and brilliantly portrayed in Allan Bloom's book, *THE CLOSING OF THE AMERICAN MIND* (Simon and Schuster, 1987). With it's magnetic subtitle, *How Higher Education Has Failed Democracy and Impoverished the Souls of Today's Students,* it was a spectacular publishing success—selling over one million copies in its first two years. Doubtless, some educators—perhaps many—continue to believe that Bloom's critique is valid even today. A retrospective is in order.

Bloom pinpoints the lack of commitment, the dearth of reflective and long-range thinking, the absence of genuine discourse, historical illiteracy, the dominance of cultural and educational relativism, and a host of psychological, philosophical and social problems in American society and culture. The reader is constantly tempted to buy the package, if only for the sparkle of the exposition. Here one must be very careful, for Bloom's analysis falls far short of a complete picture.
In terms of history and knowledge of education and public policy, the arguments and examples are narrowly based, inaccurate in certain important details, and even skewed to the political right. Seven areas of key concern lead this writer to conclude that this fascinating book, with all of its interesting approach to educational issues, is in itself a part of any closing of the American mind.

Illusory Historical Perceptions: Bloom fawns on the 1950's as a sound "golden age" preceding the unreason and terror by which he characterizes the decade following. The incitements of the 1960's (especially student revolt), according to the author, set the stage for the present malaise.

159

But Bloom's historical perception and set is illusory. The 50's were characterized by conformity and drift. It was the decade of *the man in the grey flannel suit*, and a time of doing little or nothing about grave social problems that were then building: racial segregation, colonialism and Vietnam, industrial drift as the U.S. floated relatively untouched by World War II, cold and hot war, and McCarthyism. It was also a decade known for its books and articles criticizing the sloppiness, the constraint and irrelevance of American education. The Council for Basic Education was formed to counter what historian Arthur Bestor and others saw as the aimlessness and watered-down soup of education in the U.S.

The 1950's produced considerable research into the political mentality and unconsciousness of Americans, including *The American Voter* (Campbell and Associates); *Public Opinion* (Lane and Sears); *Communism, Conformity and Civil Liberties* (Stouffer) and "Consensus and Ideology in American Politics" (McCloskey).
Added to these were psychological and sociological probes by David Riesman, Gordon Allport, C. Wright Mills, and many others whose efforts yielded the general conclusion that political ignorance, bias, lack of basic knowledge, and sheer apathy and materialism infected American society and the body politic of that decade. Although heightened by postwar escapism, these trends could be found for decades both before and after the period in question.

There is little doubt that education in the 1950's was in the doldrums, contrary to Bloom's perception. Evidence for education malaise is easily found in special studies such as the *Report of the Williamstown Workshop* and the Purdue High School Studies, the latter involving huge national samples of student opinion. Popular columns and commentaries of the times reinforced expert's concerns about educational debility. Indeed, only the scare of *Sputnik* was finally enough to shock the politicians into voting federal funds for improving education. So much for Mr. Bloom's view of the 1950's as a golden time for America.

Distorted View of the Sixties: Perhaps the most striking example of political distortion in Bloom's analysis is his identification of the student ferment of the 1960's as a more contemporary manifestation of National Socialism or Nazism in Germany of the 1930's. Here he fails to recognize the object of American student protest or to understand the ethical role of a university as both a forum and an agent in the process of political dissent and change. Indeed, little does he discuss the burning issue of campus recruitment and research for the Vietnam War effort, or the nature and intellectual implications of the civil rights movement antecedent to it. Instead, he concludes that all the turbulence was related to thuggery and a storm-trooper mentality, or that it was just revolt for the sake of disruption.

American universities were involved as feeder agents for the military adventurism of that time, and the war in Vietnam, now commonly viewed as a huge and costly blunder, posed a distinct moral challenge to both the young and the university. Would Bloom have preferred that the universities sit back and do nothing, even aid and abet that devastating war, as did occur in Nazi Germany?

The students literally had their lives on the line, with service draft calls steadily increasing. And had it not been for student protest and university teach-ins, it is questionable if the war would have wound down. By the same token, it was university activists who led much of the successful effort at gaining voting and other civil rights for besieged minorities in the South and elsewhere.

There were great disruptions and extremist behavior, of course, including participation in drugs and cults and even violence. But revolutions are by nature not tidy affairs. While simultaneously the hippie-students are criticized for not taking education seriously, Bloom and his fellow critics take the social activists to task for taking their university education *too seriously*!

The failure of German universities in the 1930's to stand up for freedom was a desertion of morality and taught a painful lesson to a society with a supposed high culture. Indeed, Bloom might well have loved teaching the clean-cut, non-protesting, and obedient students of Nazi Germany, save that he too would have had to pass muster under the Nuremberg codes. That American students and American universities took that lesson of history to heart and challenged the right and authority of the government to pursue what was seen as an unjust and undeclared war is not a cause for disdain, but is a reason for pride and hope.

Allan Bloom completely missed this lesson The university protests and teach-ins of the 1960's may well prove the real "golden age" of the 20th century, while the conformity, self-centeredness and blind materialism of the present era more likely mirrors the 1950's, which Bloom mistakenly idealizes.

Failure to Understand Economic Realities: Bloom's ties to the "trickle-down" capitalism of the University of Chicago economic "school" is bothersome. His book on American education grew out of an article he wrote for William Buckley's *National Review.* Bloom has a right to his elitist view, but his bias is everywhere evident. His philosophizing about "the good old days" and their verities reflects rugged individualism and ivory tower utopia. Blooms' carping criticism fails to adequately deal with realities of economic and social life in the latter half of the 20th century: the interdependence of the planet both ecologically and economically; the failure of laissez faire as an economic prescription for the maladies of most nations; the powerful influences of technological change. He fails to see that any lack of idealism and commitment of today's young to his concept of order in good part stems from rebellion against the dulling conformity and materialism of the times.

Commitment to high principles and public good, and to a fully examined life, cannot grow from belief in the concept of god as a conservative and conforming businessman, educator, or politician—not even from those who read the Great Books, as selected by professor Bloom.

The young, for better or for worse, have awakened to the hollowness of *noblesse oblige;* many have also awakened to the emptiness of both television and authoritarian-administrator role models.

Value Questions: Values are not discovered by reason, says Bloom, and thus it is fruitless to find the truth or the good life on that value path. Yet, values *are* based on assumptions of fact, and it is these assumptions that are open to exploration, research, and questioning. Otherwise, just whose values shall be supreme?...and who shall judge?

The relativism that Bloom decries is based upon a failure to deal with value questions. In education, the trend is to avoid such problems through mathematical gyrations done in the name of science. That is indeed a failure of the university, particularly of those practicing economics and social science by trying to reduce human problems and issues to numbers. Cross-disciplinary perspective is essential to staying clear of such blind alleys. The problem of the compartmentalized approach, one which avoids basic value questions, cannot be resolved in a segmented curriculum—however issues of value are "scientifically" examined and reduced to computer logic.

Elitism at the Expense of Egalitarianism: As James Madison warned, it is dangerous to exalt order at the cost of liberty. Bloom is afraid that too much liberty yields a climate of egalitarianism in which standards fall even as civil commotion increases. But is the remedy for falling standards more elitism and restricting access to higher education? The Jeffersonian answer is *more* education, a direction far preferable in a proven historical sense than rule by supposed intellectual elites. The element of snobbery runs strong in Allan Bloom's rule.

European Realities: Hearkening back to Europe as the center of culture and the source of American idealism is carried to the extreme. It was from Europe that the refugees poured to American shores, and it was in that Europe that the stew of elitism, class rivalry, feudalism, and modern war was spawned. This is not to overlook Europe's fantastic cultural achievements or her gifts to America. But we should not be carried away by Bloom's glorification of the old world.

The chapter on Weimar Germany, for example, is distorted. Here Bloom finds political extremism and disruptive behavior as a function of "liberalism". Extremist politics and a pandering to the lowest tastes did occur, along with a cultural renaissance. But extremist behavior in Weimar grew our of social and economic desperation following World War I. It was a flight from reality brought on by the total disruption created in the breakdown of the old imperial order. And there was an inability to implant a healthy society in the face of crushing burdens of debt imposed by the victors and the European system. The political right, not the liberals, profited from that. Indeed, disruptions and chaotic breakdown were conditions precedent to the rise of the Nazis.

In a parallel vein, the selfishness and violence one finds in American society today are not functions of liberalism, but of the failure of this society to have a consistent definition of public service and public good. What rules today, despite some healthy exceptions, is an ethic of greed and selfishness that under-girds this era of debt and "making it" and "having it all *now*". And that leaves little room or hope of long range responsibility and investment for the public good. The young, over whom Bloom wrings his hands, only reflect the values of the older generation.

Higher Education as a Gentlemanly Art: I do not quarrel with Bloom's criticism of higher education as a kind of cafeteria pandering to any and every special interest allied with careerism. While there is serious need for common learnings, these should not wholly be dictated by classical texts. The really important issue relates to the underlying problems of over-specialization, and a consequent compart-mentalization of higher education. In post-industrial society, the core learnings must focus on ecological awareness, global perspectives, and sane policies for cop-ing with shrinking resources on a beleaguered planet. Education cannot afford to fixate on the classical *trivium* (grammar, rhetoric and logic) or make a fetish of chronological survey courses and pedantic texts that have made so much of tradi-tional university education a hurdle-jumping status game. So narrowly focused, education becomes a futile exercise, often one of gentlemanly polish and pursuits which lead to pomposity rather than caring or commitment or even efficiency.

Bloom seems more concerned with maintaining the symbols of education, an elitism of the "truly educated" as distinguished from the masses—complete with snobbish schools, clubs, and lots of hubris; it is the old "old boy" set with an aca-demic degree as a license to sneer. And that is exactly the prescription for disaster, as brilliantly described in David Halberstam's analysis of the failure of leadership during the Vietnam war (*The Best and the Brightest*), and in the tragedy of the space shuttle *Challenger* (and now *Columbia*) with its arrogant "leave it to the experts"—to say nothing of the bad habit of playing the game so as not to chal-lenge or offend dumb authority. The 21st century brings again crises in the mar-ketplace as a function of huge corporations lacking concern for employees while giving huge bonuses to executives, and brazenly "cooking the books."

Allan Bloom's *The Closing of the American Mind* does make for great copy and exciting reading. His message is hardly new, however. Every ten to fifteen years it is played out again by decrying the younger generation. Each generation feels superior by virtue of bragging rights about the "good old days" when they got *real education.*
Like the war veterans who idealize their military experience years later, they forget the battlefield realities. Now it is all wine and glory. Bloom bathes in illusions of grandeur about a past that never was quite the way he sees it. He offers few pre-scriptions for educational change that deal with planetary realities or the diverse nature of modern society. He is more compartmentalized than those he criticizes, and he tries to cloud the issues. The problems of war and peace, of poverty and ecology, of multinational corporations and American hegemony, the pains of the Third World and the arms race, largely fomented or abetted by the great powers, cannot really be addressed and resolved by focusing on the training of a supposed elite for leadership. It's been tried before with often tragic consequences.

History reveals that elites become inbred and arrogant and suckers for power and control and a self-anointed snobbery. In that trap Bloom has woven his web. And the real tragedy is that so many educated people have been taken in by his book that purports to demonstrate how higher education has failed democracy and impoverished the souls of today's students.

To the contrary, if education has failed democracy it is by adopting some of the worst aspects of corporate rigidity, economic greed and selfishness. Fixated on grants, it so often fails to see, promote, and reward teaching as both art and science—as is true of the society at large. By failing in good part to nourish the critical mind, to emphasize long range and imaginative thinking and a basic commitment to stewardship of the planet as a first priority, it folds in on itself and loses much of its creative potential.

Yet, we have seen that education can be and to some extent is, in some quarters, a powerful catalyst for reform. Let us hope the **real** reformers will not only grow in number and in compelling vigor, but that they will turn the direction and force of our educational system away from an industrial model and the endless re-setting of flowery long range goals. Instead, let us move toward changing functional priorities and, in so doing, make the educational system much more effective. We must move critically and courageously in order to prevail.

Bibliography—The Education Mirage

CHAPTER 1:. Robert E. Lane and David O. Sears. *PUBLIC OPINION* (Englewood Cliffs, New Jersey) Prentice Hall, Inc., 1964, pp. 69-70.

Ira Winn. "Facts Are Not the Answer," presentation at the Alexander Meiklejohn Convocation, University of Wisconsin, Madison: in CULTURAL LITERACY AND THE CORE CURRICULUM (Sonoma, CA) Arcus Pub. 1991, pp. 51-56

C. Trosset: "Obstacles to Open Discussion and Critical Thinking: The Grinnell College Study," CHANGE, V.30, No. 5, September-Octobetr 1998, pp.44-49.

Irving Stone. CLARENCE *DARROW FOR THE DEFENSE* (New York., N.Y.) Bantam Books, Inc. 1958, page 7.

CHAPTERS 2 and 3: none

CHAPTER 4: Edna St. Vincent Millay. untitled sonnet (commonly known as "Upon This Gifted Age") in *COLLECTED SONNETS of EDNA St. VINCENT MILLAY (*New York, N.Y.) Harper and Row, 1941, page 140.

CHAPTERS 5-6: none

CHAPTER 7: "Wilderness in Silence" adapted from Ira J. Winn: SAN LUIS OBISPO COUNTY TRIBUNE, MAY 9,1998, p. B9.

CHAPTER 8: John I. Goodlad. *A PLACE CALLED SCHOOL.* (New York, N.Y.) McGraw-Hill, 1984).

CHAPTER 9: case 3: from letters to THE LOS ANGELES TIMES, (edited and paraphrased) November 13 and 24, 1984.

CHAPTER 10: Gregory Farrington quoted in Martha Woodall: "Learning Curve Now Eternal," *KNIGHT RIDDER*/SAN LUIS OBISPO COUNTY TRIBUNE. March 20, 2000, page B5

C. Peck *et. al.* "Techno-Promoter Dreams, Student Realities," PHI DELTA KAPPAN, V.83, No. 6, February 2002, pp. 472-480.

CHAPTER 11: Diane Ravich, Theodore R. Sizer *et. al.* (article and rebuttals) "Education After the Culture Wars," DAEDALUS, v.131, No. 3, Summer, 2002, pp. 5-45 +.

Ira Winn: "High School Reform: Stuffing the Turkeys," PHI DELTA KAPPAN v.65, November, 1983, pp. 184-185

G. W. Bracey: "The Forgotten 42%," PHI DELTA KAPPAN, V.80, No. 9 May 1999, pp. 7-12.

Neil Postman: *THE END OF EDUCATION* (New York, N.Y.) Penguin (USA) 1986. Also: *AMUSING OURSELVES TO DEATH*. (New York, N.Y.) Alfred A. Knopf, 1996.

Ira Winn: "Put Reformers on Hold: Tend your Garden, "THE EXECUTIVE EDUCATOR, 11, #4, April, 1989, page 52.

Ira Winn. "A Course in Defense of Public Education,: EDUCATION WEEK, V, #20, January 29, 1986, page 14.

Thomas J. Peters & Robert A. Waterman, Jr. *IN SEARCH OF EXCELLENCE: LESSONS FROM AMERICA'S BEST RUN COMPANIES,* (New York, N.Y.) Warner Books Edition, 1982 See also: Jim Collins. *GOOD TO GREAT: WHY SOME COMPANIES MAKE THE LEAP...AND OTHERS DON'T* (New York, N.Y.) HarperCollins, 2001

CHAPTER 12: Ira J. Winn, "Critical Consciousness in Adult Education," INTERNATIONAL REVIEW OF EDUCATION,37 (3) 1991: pp381-384 UNESCO Institute for Education. Included therein quotes from: Angus Campbell and Associates, *THE AMERICAN VOTER.* (New York: John Wiley & Sons, Inc. 1964); Mortimer Adler, "Why Only Adults Can Be Educated" in R. Gross, ed., *INVITATION TO LIFELONG EDUCATION* (Chicago: Follett Pub, 1982); C. Hartley Gratton, *IN QUEST OF KNOWLEDGE* (New York: Association Press, 1955). Ira J. Winn: "Dimensions of Political Unconsciousness," *INTERNATIONAL YEARBOOK.* (Band XI, Braunschweig Textbook Institute,

Germany (UNESCO) 1967),pp. 35-53. John Ohliger and David Lisman, "Must We All Go Back to School?", PROGRESSIVE, 42, No. 10, October, 1978, pp. 36-37.

CHAPTER 13: Ira Winn: "A Tale of Double Vision" PHI DELTA KAPPAN, 72, #9, May l991, pp. 711-712.

Ira Winn: "Lamenting Teacher Training": Adapted from: "Teaching Armies of the Damned," EDUCATIONAL HORIZONS 65, #2, Winter l987, pp. 83-84

C.D. Glickman: "Dichotomizing Education: Why No One Wins and America Loses," PHI DELTA KAPPAN, V.53, No. 2, October, 2001, pp. 147-152.

CHAPTER 14: "At the Core of Higher Education," adapted from: Ira Winn, "Civilizing the Dialogue in the Forgetting Society," PHI DELTA KAPPAN, 70, No. 8, April 1989, pp. 630-631.

"The Environment of Reform" adapted from: Ira J. Winn, "Ecology and the University," PHI DELTA KAPPAN, LIII, No. 3, November, 1981, pp. 156-159.

I. H. Buchen: "Education in America: The Next 25 Years," THE FUTURIST, v. 37, No. 1, January-February 2003, pp. 44-50.

D. Posner: "Education for the 21st Century," PHI DELTA KAPPAN, 84, No. 4, December 2002, pp. 316-317.

Raymond Nace. "Arrogance Toward Landscape" Bulletin of The Atomic Scientist, Dec. 1969, pp. 11-14.

AUTHOR CONTACT: educationmirage@ yahoo.com

INFORMATION AND BOOK ORDERS

iUniverse.com
click: search bookstore

Or: Amazon.com Or other bookstores

0-595-29142-2

Made in the USA
Lexington, KY
01 October 2010